PASSION RULES!
Inspiring Women in Business

Alexandra Powe Allred

edited by
Constance C. Dickinson

The Oasis Press®/ PSI Research
Central Point, Oregon

Published by The Oasis Press®
© 2000 by Alexandra Powe Allred

This publication is designed to provide accurate and authoritative information in regard to the subject matter covered. It is sold with the understanding that the publisher is not engaged in rendering legal, accounting, or other professional service. If legal advice or other expert assistance is required, the services of a competent professional person should be sought.
— from a declaration of principles jointly adopted by a committee of the American Bar Association and a committee of publishers.

Managing editor: Constance C. Dickinson
Assistant editor and compositor: Jan Olsson
Book designer: Constance C. Dickinson
Cover designer: J. C. Young

Please direct any comments, questions, or suggestions regarding this book to The Oasis Press®/PSI Research:

Editorial Department
P.O. Box 3727
Central Point, OR 97502
(541) 245-6502
info@psi-research.com *e-mail*

The Oasis Press® is a Registered Trademark of Publishing Services, Inc., an Oregon corporation doing business as PSI Research.

Allred, Alexandra Powe, 1965–
    Passion rules! : inspiring women in business / Alexandra Powe Allred ; edited by Constance C. Dickinson.
        p. cm. — (PSI successful business library)
    Includes bibliographical references and index.
    ISBN 1-55571-530-3
    1. Women executives—United States—Case studies. 2. Women-owned business enterprises—United States—Case studies. 3. Success in business—United States—Case studies. 4. Inspiration. I. Title. II. Series.

HD6054.4.U6 P68 2000
658.4'09'082—dc21   00-056669

Printed in the United States of America
First edition 10 9 8 7 6 5 4 3 2 1

Printed on recycled paper when available.

To Penny, the little voice in my ear,
and all those who love her

Contents

——

Foreword

—

When Alex Powe Allred asked me to write the forward to this book, my first thought was that I wasn't a writer. This brought back memories of what I said seven years ago when I started my first company: "I couldn't possibly start a business, I am not an entrepreneur." Then I realized what this book was all about — success through passion, not necessarily through knowledge or former experience. Seven years ago, I didn't know how to write press releases, business plans, or ad campaigns. I just did it. That's the key message in this book. Once women get in touch with their passion for what it is they are creating and their inner strength, nothing can stop them from becoming successful entrepreneurs.

Passion Rules! could not be a better title for a book on women entrepreneurs. We must follow our hearts, even when it means we must sometimes disregard rules set by others to do so. Breaking rules often leads to innovations and innovations make entrepreneurs. Honor, self-worth, and respect are found when you follow your heart.

This may be the reason women are starting their own businesses like never before in American history. Tired of hitting their heads on glass ceilings, women are building businesses without ceilings, without limits. Women-owned businesses have more than doubled in the last twelve years, totaling 9.1 million businesses and accounting for thirty-eight percent of all businesses in this country. Women owned businesses are generating $3.6 trillion annually and employing more than twenty-seven million Americans.

Not only are women contributing to our country's economic growth, we are redefining success. In the old paradigm of business, success equaled money individually amassed, and power meant power over others. Women see these two concepts in a fundamentally different way. Money becomes our tool for independence, to follow our passions and to build sustainable and healthy lifestyles. Power is more about our inner strength to overcome obstacles and to use our resources to make the world a better place. This book demonstrates a revolution in the making.

It is first and foremost a personal revolution. Women are asking themselves, "What am I passionate about? What is my purpose? What is my true calling?" We all have a purpose. It is through our innate gifts that we may express this purpose, and it is our passion that leads us there. Finding our passion and having the courage to follow it is critical to becoming a successful entrepreneur. The joy in following our passion allows us to tirelessly overcome obstacles. The women in this book candidly share some of the obstacles they themselves have overcome with hope you may learn from their mistakes — I would be lying if I said there were not many on the path of an entrepreneur. The difference is when you are working at what you love, it hardly seems like work.

This personal revolution takes on new meaning when we let our values lead our businesses. From this new definition of work, we awaken our creative self-expression and, as a result, we awaken our self-worth. The feminine way to create business is about nurturing and growing our vision so it becomes much larger than the individual and becomes a driving force for positive change in the world. Women entrepreneurs have realized creating values-led businesses not only feels good, it is also a smart business model.

Personal success becomes a protocol for our collective success. As we succeed, we give back. Jennifer Maxwell, through her company Power-Bar, has donated more than $260,000 to grassroots organizations that ensure trails and waterways remain protected for public use. Jenny Craig of Jenny Craig Weight Management Centers has donated over $20 million for improving education in this country. In my first company, we started a program in which employees were able to volunteer one day a month at a non-profit organization of their choice while being paid as if they were at work.

Women-owned businesses are also instituting programs like flex time, family leave, and alternative healthcare programs because they know that balancing work and family is no small feat. Placing a value on balance is a new idea propagated by women entrepreneurs. It is proving to be much better for the employee, the company, and the bottom line in the long term.

Sharing our experiences and expertise with each other is an integral part of this emerging smart business model. I call it the Old Girl's Network. Our individual power becomes our collective strength when we join forces and support one another. This book is a wonderful example of propagating women's networking. You will learn the importance of teamwork, communication, and networking. These are skills women naturally possess. When they are transferred to the business environment, they become invaluable assets. You will feel the passion from the women in this book, learn from their successes and failures, and learn how and why women run businesses differently. Get ready because their passion is contagious.

Eleanor Roosevelt said, "The future belongs to those who believe in the beauty of their dreams." Believe in your dreams, let your passion rule, and you too can join the revolution of successful women entrepreneurs.

Wishing you success on your terms,

Jenai Lane
President and CEO of Zeal, Company

Preface

In the course of many of my meetings with top businesswomen, I was often asked about my own background in business. Initially, I was tentative with my answer. By trade, I am a writer who simply loves to relay a great tale. Had I lived in ancient times, I like to think I would have been Gabrielle, faithful sidekick to Xena, warrior princess — loyal, trustworthy, fairly athletic, compassionate, and a darned-good story-teller. Earlier in my life, I was an athlete — in fact, that's how the writer in me was truly awakened. As a member of the U.S. Women's Bobsled team, I lived for a brief period at the Olympic Training Center in Lake Placid, New York. But this was embarrassing information to share with such business giants as Jenny Craig, Jennifer Maxwell, and Debbi Fields Rose. Instead, I played up the little hands-on business experience I had. Together, my father and I designed The Challenger, an electronic challenge and response security system used to verify that security guards are alert and coherent.

This idea's genesis was in Moscow, Russia. My father was assigned to the U.S. Embassy as a military attaché. I spent a lot of time in the embassy where I often saw the U.S. Marine security guards carrying a large round clock as they made their patrols through the embassy compound. The clock, known as the Detex Watch Clock and invented more than 100 years ago, required the Marine on duty to stop at key stations, then insert and turn the numbered key in the clock in order to prove that he was where he was supposed to be at the time he was supposed to be there. I was fascinated by that clock, even though I didn't have a clue about its importance.

Years later, after retiring from the military, my father became a security consultant for an international organization. In his travels around the world, usually to places in great need of security, places where property and lives were (and still are) in more or less constant danger, he often found that security staff and property were routinely threatened by guards falling asleep or getting drunk. Too often they were getting themselves and others killed. In fact, four years after our patent, Princess Diana was killed due to the actions of a driver who should have had to take The Challenger test before getting behind the wheel.

While our invention was developed from a desire to meet a need, I did not start my entrepreneurial career with such ideologies. I was consumed with the idea of inventing something that would earn the big bucks I wanted. However, life has a way of moving you along unexpected pathways. It was a few years before my inventor's spirit had a chance to break out again. In my late teens and early twenties, I had opted out of college — for a few years, anyway — and worked as a dog trainer. For four years, I did basic obedience, a little show training, advance training, and consultations. During this time I had what seemed like a brilliant idea.

A major complaint of many pet owners was that their dogs climbed on the furniture when left alone at home. The dog training school where I worked was pretty upscale, and most of our clientele — Senator Bob Dole and Elizabeth Dole and cosmetic giant Estee Lauder, to drop a few names — were quite wealthy and had very nice furniture. They didn't appreciate the everyday wear and tear of puppies jumping and rolling around on their sofas, chairs, and beds.

What to do? Without going into the finer details, I invented the perfect solution. I talked to my boss about it and even sketched it out for him. He loved the idea. Then, I proceeded to talk about it for another three and a half years. One day, I was on a plane flipping through one of those nifty, expensive airline catalogues that are in the seat pockets. To my horror, I discovered a very similar device "just out on the market." I'd put off taking action on my idea for too long.

Entrepreneur Joy Mangano shares a similar experience. She sat on an invention for several years — too embarrassed to show it to others — only to have it "reinvented" by someone else and sold on the market for a pretty penny. She swore she would never let that happen again. Mangano now sits on the million-dollar trademark for the Miracle Mop.

Great ideas require action — something I had yet to learn. It was not until 1994 that I stumbled into something all-consuming, something for which I had so much passion I didn't mind not making any money. Ironically, every successful businessperson I've talked with has identified the basic element of success as the *passion*, not the money. My passion was, of all things, bobsledding. Now I understand why business book after business book use sports analogies to explain strategies, formulas for success, and leadership abilities. Betty Harrigan, who championed women in business in her best-seller *Games Mother Never Taught You*, claimed that women needed to incorporate sports thinking into the business mindset in order to succeed.

I didn't take a risk with the anti-furniture dog device. I wasn't a visionary or a realist in my earlier quests focused on making the big bucks. I lacked passion, dedication, and a full understanding of what is involved in being successful in business. I had this preconceived notion that to become an entrepreneur was very risky business. I was afraid that it would cost more to start than I could ever afford, so I let my idea sit. Maybe a pile of money would just fall into my lap.

Bobsledding changed all that. It challenged me, not just physically, but spiritually; it stirred real passions in me. And, strange though it may seem, it is the men who opposed women bobsledders I can thank for unintentionally spurring me on.

Because women in this sport were not allowed in the Olympics, it became my mission to change things. Fortunately, after many years of hard campaigning, women's bobsledding has finally been included in the 2002 Salt Lake City Games.

I trained, busted my rear-end, annoyed my husband, drained the time and energy of my parents, defied all the odds, and not only made the first U.S. Women's Bobsled Team but, when four months pregnant, won the gold medal in the U.S. Nationals. After that, I was benched till I had the baby. While my nonpregnant teammates went on to train, I went to work building the support system needed for women sledders.

Author showing off her gold medal
after the 1994 U.S. Nationals

The U.S. Bobsled Federation, a seemingly natural ally, made it very clear they had no time for the women's team. They had no one in their office who could help us; they had no equipment for us, no coaching staff, no public relations officer. In truth, the men's team was understaffed and underfunded, so there was nothing with which to support the women's team. We were on our own. In the next two years, I became the team leader, spokesperson, public relations officer, manager, editor of the women's bobsled newsletter, and foreign correspondent to Canada, Germany, England, Switzerland, and Latvia.

During the 1995–96 season, I went to work looking for funding, getting our first team uniforms and, eventually, finding a real honest-to-goodness financial consultant who was able to bring in the big dollars that were needed for travel and sleds.

I learned a lot about budgeting, public relations, writing and creating press kits, contacting the press, and selling a team. The team was my product. I co-authored the guidelines for the women's bobsled program. I learned, also, how to campaign to the International Olympic Committee (IOC), International Federation of Bobsledding and Tobogganing (FIBT), U.S. Olympic Committee (USOC), and our own federation. I became a teacher, spending hours and hours explaining USOC, IOC, and federation policy to teammates. I became a realist about policy. I became a risk-taker, an alliance builder, and even a role model. And each time I was told this was never going to happen, each time we had what sparse equipment we owned taken away and given to the men's "B" team, each time we were cut out of funding, I became that much more determined.

Actually, I was a mediocre bobsledder. I did quite well in the beginning, but those were the early years. Bigger and better women were coming along. My efforts were not about my making the Olympics. They were about fighting for what was right.

I learned a lot from those bobsledding days. Perhaps the most important lesson I learned was about team players. It was a hard lesson. I learned about women who would sell you out for a chance to appear on television, if only for a few moments. I learned about team players whose word was their bond and about others who did not understand the concept of honor. It was an intense, four year roller coaster ride with lots of highs and lows. But, as one businesswoman after another assured me, if you can learn from those lows and from the errors you make along the way, you can be a winner.

Isn't it funny an ex-dog trainer and bobsledder should fall into the world of business because of those vocations. Initially, I was embarrassed to tell other businesswomen about my indirect route to the business world. I shouldn't have been. In fact, very few businesswomen I spoke with followed traditional, business-school paths to success. For example, J'Amy Owens of The Retail Group, dubbed the "Sales Guru to the Stars," has no formal background in business. Yet, she is an authority on how to create a business and one of the most powerful women in the retail industry, with clients such as Disney, M&M/Mars, Blockbuster Video, and Starbucks — and she's not alone.

Who would have thought an ex-dolphin trainer could open a cookie store and turn it into a multi-million dollar franchise? Who would expect a cabbie to make and sell signature pillows or an ex-ballerina to manufacture and sell soap? What might an ex-skeleton athlete know about high finance or a keypunch operator about the bakery business? What would a lawyer know about the flyfishing business? Yet, as you will read, all these women successfully made the transition to successful businesswomen and are living proof that passion rules.

Right now there is a woman somewhere, maybe you, with an incredible idea who is held back by the notion she hasn't the needed experience. Maybe, she's thinking, all she knows is child care, bowling, or knitting. Maybe her claim to fame is making a mean macaroni salad and, for that reason alone, she is mortified to tell anyone she is thinking about opening a muffler shop.

If that woman is you, don't stop yourself from living your dream because you don't think you have the necessary experience. All of the women you will read about in this book were able to draw upon their unique life experiences to bring something special and different to their business. This book was written because of my own experiences with the round-about ways to success. You'll be surprised by what you actually know. And what you don't know, you can begin to learn from the following pages.

Passion Rules! is filled with stories you won't find in other business books because it is highly personal and relates to women of the new millennium. The list of terrific, innovative, and exciting women who share their stories with us is startling. It is amazing that so many of them promptly returned telephone calls or set up luncheon dates to talk about their successes, what went wrong, the unanticipated calamities, and how they turned those misfortunes into the learning opportunities on which they built their successful businesses and lives. They share funny, embarrassing, heartwarming stories about their teams — family, friends, and co-workers.

I cannot describe what a pleasure it was to talk with each and every one of these women and just how seriously they take their roles of mentor, role-model, friend, and businesswoman. What I hope for is that their words and stories will inspire you and lead you on your own successful journey, wherever that may take you.

Once inspired, you will be able to take your next steps by using some of the resources provided in the back of the book. There are several organizations listed alphabetically and described that exist to assist women entrepreneurs. Also, several books are described so you can choose those pertinent to achieving your dream.

May your journey be an exciting and fulfilling adventure.

Introductions

T here's no greater inspiration or guide for striving to achieve one's dreams than someone who has succeeded in achieving theirs. You are about to meet several women who, due to their passion, diligence, and creativity, have created businesses and have succeeded in making their dreams come true. And along the way, they have contributed greatly to the benefit of others. Some are from big cities while others are from small towns. What these women have in common is passion. The kind of passion one needs to make it in the business world is something within you; it can't be learned.

Linda Katz

What started out as an amusing family website turned into a passion and a successful business for Linda Katz. In fact, Katz' virtual store, Prairie Tumbleweed Farm, was used as a model for a perfect business by Richard A. Bendis when he spoke to the graduating class of Kansas State University School of Business.

Katz wanted to create a website for her family. She had no idea how to make one, but she taught herself how to create and design web pages, bought a digital camera, took some amusing pictures of her family cultivating tumbleweeds, and voilà. Prairie Tumbleweed Farm was born. As you will read, Katz was not prepared for the worldwide response she got.

Linda Katz ~ Prairie Tumbleweed Farm

Prairie Tumbleweed Farm serves as an excellent example of "if you can conceive, you can achieve." Katz didn't fear failure. It was, after all, just a joke. Katz made use of what was around her. Because of her love for her family, her passion for trying new things, and her imagination, she was able to supply the world with tumbleweeds. Who knew there was such a great void? Who knew there were so many people in need of a good ol' tumbleweed?

Cris Dolan

How many people, women in particular, have stopped themselves short of creating a new business or designing a prototype for an invention because they didn't believe they had the right background or enough education? You must be a near genius to create a successful business, right?

Not so, says business executive Cris Dolan, MIT graduate and ex-model turned major business mogul. The keys to success do not come from having a college degree or a high I.Q., they are qualities: passion, persistence, and a willingness to take risks.

I first met the supersonic CEO of OneMain.com at the Olympic Training Center in Lake Placid, New York, of all places. Dolan was a world-class skeleton athlete. Whipping down an icy mountain at speeds of seventy, eighty, and ninety miles per hour, skeleton athletes lie on their stomach on a small steel sled, head first, using hips and shoulders to steer while hanging on for dear life. I was there as a bobsledder but had seen enough skeleton races to ask the question, "Who in their right mind would do that?"

Although, unlike Dolan, Katz never aspired to fling herself down an icy death ride, these two women are not so different, after all. Both Katz and Dolan, with two completely different backgrounds and experiences, share passions born of ingenuity and creativity. Dolan, an engineer and business magnate, is one of the most sought after businesswomen in her on-line field. Unlike Katz, there's never been a day of uncertainty in Dolan's life as to whether she was going to be wildly successful or how she was going to get there.

Cris Dolan ~ OneMain.com

Dolan embraces all aspects of the business world, including failure: something she doesn't experience often, but wears like a badge of honor. In fact, on the day I first met her, I noticed she had a deep bruise on her inner left thigh. When I asked her about it, she looked down at her leg, surprised at first, and then laughed, "Oh, that." It was a battle wound from an international competition in which she turned too hard and flipped over in the curve of a ten-foot wall. When she was slammed back down to the floor of the curve, the sled came down on her, delivering a pounding so brutal she would have the bruise for more than a year. She was not afraid to get back on the sled, as so many athletes are after an experience like that. The bruise was a reminder of how to ride that particular track.

Dolan lives by a philosophy I learned from my mother. Mistakes do not equal failure. Failure is to be expected. It is a part of life that should be embraced as a learning opportunity rather than feared.

Terry Neece

This same philosophy made lobbyist Terry Neece one of the most powerful and successful businesswomen in America today. The founder of Terry Neece Personnel Services, Neece made a mistake that could have cost her her business. She did not realize how local politics could affect her business. Instead, she forged ahead, determined not only to be a success but to help other women who found themselves in a similar position. Once desperate to find a way to provide for her family, her remarkable story illustrates the value of passion. Neece made history in 1990 when she was nominated by a major political party for Lt. Governor of Oklahoma.

She co-founded and became President of GrassRoots Impact, a corporate and political strategy firm that represents the National Association of Women Business Owners (NAWBO), the National Association for the Self-Employed (NASE), and the National Business Association (NBA)

Terry Neece ~ Terry Neece Personnel Services and Grass Roots Impact

on Capital Hill. Neece is called on to testify before the House and Senate regarding business on a regular basis and is one of a five-person Brain Trust working with the U.S. House and Senate Committees on small businesses. No surprise, it was Neece who coined the phrase, "If you can conceive, you can achieve."

Jenai Lane

In my interviews with Jenai Lane, the jewelry and cosmetic magnate of Respect, Inc., I was thunderstruck by her openness, candor, and genuine desire to help other entrepreneurial hopefuls. Lane, now a common sight in all the who's-who in business magazines, has been honored as everything from Businesswoman of the Year and Entrepreneur of the Year to role-model. She speaks nationally to women's groups and now represents other women, using what she has learned in the business world to help establish new hopefuls.

Unlike those who move on beyond remembering their roots, this San Francisco native has never forgotten how often the proverbial door was slammed in her face and how horrible and frustrating it felt. She is determined to help others, wondering how often other women with great ideas have given up before ever getting a chance to blossom. Mentoring has become Lane's current passion.

This passion is not, however, just about mentoring businesswomen. Like specialty food leaders Cheryl Krueger-Horn and Debbie Fields, Lane feels strongly about giving back to her community. It is this philosophy some claim distinguishes women from

Jenai Lane ~ Respect, Inc. and Zeal, Company

men in business. Successful businesswomen have dedicated themselves and their businesses to giving back to the community far more often than their male counterparts.[1]

Dr. Karen Stephenson

It is the philosophy of caring for their communities and others that made working with these women and writing about their successes such a joy. They have an underlying commitment, not only to their business or product but also to the people around them — particularly, other women. Because so many of them faced some kind of discrimination, including the glass-ceiling phenomenon, most of these women believe mentoring is not only necessary, it is vital for women to become successful and prominent business leaders.

Women like Dr. Karen Stephenson of the Anderson Graduate School of Management at UCLA have been challenging the good ol' boy networks for many years, determined to see their sister entrepreneurs able to aspire to and achieve all they can. Raised in a household that taught her she could be anything she wanted to be, it never occurred to Stephenson, now in her forties, that she should or could have been anything less than successful. Therefore, Stephenson has been pushing the boundaries of what women are expected to do for years.

Earning her doctorate in anthropology, trudging through the jungles of Guatemala, facing down guerrilla soldiers, or starting her own business in Norway are simply part of the game for Stephenson.

Cecilia "Pudge" Kleinkauf

Neither did it occur to Cecilia "Pudge" Kleinkauf that starting her own flyfishing business in her forties while battling cancer — and later winning — might be a tad risky. Never mind that female flyfishing instructors neither existed nor were welcome on the rivers. She loved flyfishing and was going to do it for a living. So Kleinkauf launched into her own aggressive marketing strategy that gained immediate local response and, eventually, favorable recognition by the international flyfishing community.

Perhaps because her business was born out of the need for self-healing, Kleinkauf revels in mentoring. When she was diagnosed with cancer, she knew she wanted and

Cecilia "Pudge" Kleinkauf ~ Women's Flyfishing

needed to do something for herself. Flyfishing was the one thing that brought her tremendous happiness and peace. Now, she relishes giving that same feeling to other women.

Gretchen Leddy

Leddy entered the world of business knowing only two things: she wanted to be her own boss, and she loved to make cakes. Working as a keypunch operator in Cleveland, Ohio, Leddy became tired of working for someone else. Gretchen and her husband Bernie quickly redefined their boundaries and what they wanted in life when they received a phone call informing them that a bakery in Columbus, Ohio, was for sale. Uprooting their home and family, the Leddys showed extraordinary entrepreneurial spirit. Gretchen Leddy found she was working much longer, harder hours in the bakery than she ever did as a keypunch operator but, as she puts it, "those hours belonged to me."

Jenny Craig

Although each woman spoke in terms of a passion, some businesses were born out of a need to provide better care for their families while others were developed because of health issues. When international business leader Jenny Craig of Jenny Craig Weight Loss Centers International found her own weight climbing after her mother's death from an obesity related illness, she decided to learn more about fitness and health.

This was the innocuous, yet passionate beginning of her business empire. It was an issue so personal to her, she became obsessed with learning more and more. Her determination, self-education, and perseverance generated a multi-million dollar corporation.

Jenny Craig ~ Jenny Craig Weight Loss Centers International

Lisa Nistico

As an at-home mom, Lisa Nistico began to feel cut off and isolated. Although she believed in the importance of staying home with her children, she needed something more. "My mom is a gourmet cook, and I really love to cook," she says. It seemed reasonable that the gourmet food industry was the right business for her. She bought the already-thriving Gourmet Gifts from Valerie Coolidge then learned everything Coolidge warned her about the hard way: demanding schedules and deadlines, bookkeeping, and struggling with finicky and uncooperative chocolate. Imagine receiving an order for 7,000 chocolate spoons when your chocolate isn't cooperating. Nistico loves what she does and views the obstacles as growth opportunities.

Kristin Penta

Likewise, Kristin Penta knew even as a very young girl where her passion lay: cosmetics. Although her parents were determined she was not going to college to "major in lip gloss," Penta followed her heart and now heads Fun Cosmetics, a multi-million dollar company. Penta, like Dineh Mohajer, was filled by a passion so great no amount of talking could dissuade her.

Kristin Penta ~ Fun Cosmetics

Debbi Fields Rose

Many women become entrepreneurs because they simply can't help themselves. There is a voice that calls them into the mysterious, often scary world once dominated by men. It is a voice telling them they should be doing something, developing an idea, challenging the status quo, and making something happen. Debbi Fields, the founder and dynamic namesake of Mrs. Fields Cookies, says when she was a young girl, she knew she was special. She knew she was destined to do something. Only, she did not know what that something was. It was years before this ex-ballgirl and dolphin trainer discovered her passion was creating delicious cookies.

Debbi Fields Rose ~ Mrs. Fields Cookies

Lynette Reed

Lynette Reed understands this kind of passion. All of her friends and family tried to talk her out of pursuing her idea. It was absurd, really. How was an out-of-work model with no credit and no savings going to open up a candle shop in Los Angles? Yet, Reed's need to answer her own calling was too powerful to listen to reason. She hocked everything she owned: jewelry, furniture, and her bike to pay for the first three months rent on a small shop in West Hollywood. There was almost no money left to buy inventory. Then, Lady

Lynette Reed ~ Illume Candles, Inc.

Luck smiled, and actress Melanie Griffith walked through the door, ordered 120 gift baskets, and changed Illume Candles, Inc. forever.

Tara Cronbaugh

Luck is a powerful tool in the world of business. But knowing what to do with it is what makes a business hopeful a business magnate. For women like Lynette Reed or Linda Katz who never attended college, moving into the business world was an intimidating prospect. The idea has always been you must have a college degree to be successful. Certainly, education helps. When Tara Cronbaugh decided she wanted to open her own business, the Iowa City Coffee Company, she was already listening to

Tara Cronbaugh ~ Iowa City Coffee Company

her instinct — a yet to be clarified passion — and taking a sixteen-week course on entrepreneurialism with Ed Moldt, director of the John Papa-John Entrepreneurial Center of the University of Iowa. Before attending Moldt's course, Cronbaugh hadn't an inkling as to what a feasibility study was or what a business plan should look like. With the help of Moldt, a successful inventor, entrepreneur, and business leader, Cronbaugh was able to devise a business proposal that would later allow her to approach financial institutions for loans and credit.

Knowing what do to once you've identified that powerful feeling inside is crucial. As Debbi Fields reminds us, "Know the rules of the game."

Cozy Wolan

Even for women like Cozy Wolan, who did all the research she could on making and creating a successful hair cuttery for children, plenty of mistakes will still occur. However, she knew how to create a feasibility re-port, budget, and business plan and was able to anticipate most of the needs and trouble spots in advance for Cozy's Cuts for Kids. More important, because Wolan and the others have shared their mistakes as well as their strategies, you might be able to avoid many of the in-evitable pitfalls.

You don't need an MBA to create a successful business, but you must believe in your idea and be willing to take some risks — after you've learned how to minimize those risks.

Cozy Wolan ~ Cozy's Cuts for Kids

Dineh Mohajer

Dineh Mohajer was a twenty-year-old medical student in Los Angeles, sitting in class one day not paying attention, not listening to the profes-sor, not taking notes. She was staring at the toenails on her sandaled foot, wishing she had nail polish to match her pastel blue purse. The only nail polish colors available, she mused, were variations of red and pink. Wouldn't it be cool if nail polishes came in all colors, so women could match their nails to their clothes? Mohajer had found her passion. She dropped out of medical school to develop a line of nail polish and her own multi-million dollar corporation, Hard Candies, Inc.

Like some of the ingenious and gutsy women in this book, Mohajer was able to redefine her boundaries and what she wanted early in life. She knew that medical school didn't interest her. With passion, using her creative talents, she began creating her own prototypes to interest prospective buyers. In less than a year, Mohajer's clients included some of the biggest of the big name department stores as well as exclusive Beverly Hills boutiques.

Tess Rano

A part-time model and full-time mom, Tess Rano decided to open her own martial arts and kickboxing school, the Ernie Reyes School of Karate. Having once trained for the Junior Olympic Tae Kwon Do team in her teens, Rano returned to the martial arts to find local schools lacked the discipline and the kind of high demand once expected of this ancient art. She and her brother, Romy, shuffled their kids between parents, siblings, spouses, and each other; opened their own school; and made their dream a reality.

Recently, Rano earned a second-degree black belt. She performed in the presence of world renowned Ernie Reyes and received high praise.

Tess Rano ~ Ernie Reyes School of Karate

Stacey Center

Stacey Center is a trained ballerina with a Ph.D. in psychology. What could she possibly know about making and selling organic soaps?

Yet, like Linda Katz, Center's desire to sell something and her passion for making soap gave her the courage and desire push forward. Like Katz, Center taught herself how to create a website, and The Soap Quarry was born.

Stacey Center ~ The Soap Quarry

Diane Jacobs

Diane Jacobs ~ The Cakeworks

When art student Diane Jacobs discovered she loved to decorate cakes, she moved thousands of miles from her home in Cincinnati, Ohio, to Los Angeles to study the craft under a master baker and decorator. Putting her passion and amazing gift as an artist to work, Jacobs soon mastered the art and bought her own bakery, The Cakeworks. It was not long before this virtual unknown headed up a clientele list with some of the biggest names in Hollywood.

This was a bold move for Jacobs, as was Leddy's launch of a new business in a new city. Yet, as Ed Moldt explains, "You know a lot more than you think. Once you define what your boundaries are, you usually find you are not as constrained as you initially think."

Jennifer Maxwell

The former CEO of PowerBar, Inc., Jennifer Maxwell, is one of the most powerful businesswomen around and the mother of five, yes, five children. How this slim, ath-letic woman divides herself among husband, children, business, and sport is an amazing balancing act few would dare attempt. Recently, she sold PowerBar to the food giant, Nestlé Foods, but she remains active in the community.

As is the case with many of the business leaders in this book, Maxwell is committed to the idea that big businesses must take some responsibility in their communities. Under Maxwell, PowerBar donated hundreds of thousands of dol-

Jennifer Maxwell ~ PowerBar, Inc.

lars to preserve natural dirt trails for hiking, jogging, and biking. The idea of PowerBar was born from passion — her passion to compete as an athlete. And, as the business became a sound success, her passion continued, shift-ing focus from "How can I help athletes perform better?" to "How can I share my love of sports and the outdoors with others?"

Sheli Hanson

This hilarious, gregarious woman breaks every stereotype about women in business. Hanson entered the business world like a Texas tornado. A high school drop-out and one-time welfare recipient, Hanson made up her mind to change her life. She ran successful port-a-potty and septic tank businesses — "In our business, a flush is better than a full house" — in central Texas. Now she has a cattle and chicken

Sheli Hanson ~ hogwild!

ranch and a new business setting hog prints in authentic Texas red clay and selling them on the Internet. As one resident says of Hanson, "No one stands in her way. We all know better."

Cheryl Krueger-Horn

Cheryl Krueger-Horn ~ Cheryl&Co.

Krueger-Horn's entrance into the business world was not an easy one. There were personal tragedies, faulty equipment, missed deadlines, and near bankruptcy. But, today Cheryl&Co. has projected sales of more than $30 million for 2000 and is growing all the time.

When it comes to family, Krueger-Horn, understands about personal sacrifice. A strong, independent woman, this business leader talks openly about how success in business can often cause strife in personal relationships. Krueger-Horn, like Maxwell, is committed to giving back to her community. Just one of the many community projects she created is a bring-your-child-to-work program for children of local orphanages.

Jennifer Floren

Jennifer Floren graduated from an Ivy-League school, had all the right connections, had a bright future, and was ready to live out her dream until she realized her dream was not quite right. Like many college graduates, Floren was suddenly faced with the unpleasant notion that she was doing something she really didn't want to do. And like so many women before her, she was not quite sure what she could do about it until her sister asked for help finding a job.

Suddenly, her passion found her. With her extraordinary networking skills and an extensive Rolodex, Floren seemed to be the natural ally of job hunters. Thus, Ivy Productions, a professional guidance and counseling service was born. But Floren was not content to sit back on her successful laurels. As the company grew, Ivy Productions expanded into the magazine business, linking with colleges across the country for career counseling.

Named one of the women to watch by *Working Woman* magazine, Floren exemplifies the notion that women can make great risk-takers.

Jennifer Floren ~ Ivy Productions

J'Amy Owens

Linda Katz of the Prairie Tumbleweed Farm revealed that she once thought only those who graduated from college with a degree in business had license to step into the business world. If that were true, only women like Cris Dolan, Jennifer Floren, and Tara Cronbaugh would be destined for success.

Well, J'Amy Owens had nothing on paper to indicate she would become one of the most powerful women in the retail business. With no formal training in retail, unemployed and broke, Owens reinvented herself with nothing but passion, confidence, and persistence. Now, with clients such as NIKE and Blockbuster, Owens is one of the most sought after consultants in the retail business.

J'Amy Owens ~ The Retail Group

Annalisa Mastroianni

Annalisa Mastroianni was "the best damn waitress you ever had," but she quit her job as a waitress to start her own catering business, Annie's Edibles. Mastroianni prepares nutritionally balanced and individualized meals — catering to the nutritional needs of each client — and delivers them to the doorstep of her clients, who include some of the biggest names in Hollywood.

Diane Slater and Helen Yee

While living in the Olympic Training Center in Colorado Springs, Colorado, Slater and Yee saw first-hand how well massage therapy worked for athletes. Yee was on the U.S. Tae Kwon Do team and Slater was an all-state champion in the sport. They realized there was an immediate need for massage therapy for people who wanted to stay in top form or were recovering from an injury. They enrolled in a course to learn the art of massage therapy and found their passion. As Slater explains, "We didn't know what we were in for. We just sort of stumbled into something, but we knew we loved it." Before 1990, these two athletes had never even had a massage. Eight years later the pair owned a thriving business, operated the state-regulated massage therapy school they created, and were named "Rising Stars" in *CEO* magazine.[2]

As more and more women gain the confidence to throw their hats into the business ring, there will be more opportunities for women who are willing to share the ups and downs of their success to serve as role models and mentors to their friends, sisters, mothers, and daughters. These women demonstrate it is possible to wear many hats and still live out a dream. They are committed to the idea of paying back. "It is," Fields says, "a social responsibility."

You can imagine the possibilities when more women, who've been assisted with their passions and their dreams, add to the efforts of their predecessors by supporting other women's efforts and offering the fruits of their passions to benefit their employees, communities, and the world beyond. As Pamela Gilberd, author of *The Eleven Commandments of Wildly Successful Women* says, "Women's economic creativity is one of the best kept secrets in business today."[3] The women in this book and many others aim to change that.

Chapter 1

Follow Your Passion

—

Cheryl Krueger-Horn's first stab at the business world came when she was only seven years old. Filling her grandmother's pie tins with mud and strategically placing stones around the pies to look like nuts, Krueger-Horn stood on the side of a dirt road near her farmhouse in northern Ohio selling pies. To this day, the fifty-something cookie magnate is surprised by her early success. She says in amazement, "People actually bought them for a penny apiece." Krueger-Horn has had many successes since the mud pies, and she has worked hard to achieve them. A born entrepreneur, her life story is one of overcoming difficulties, seizing opportunities, and sharing rewards. How did she get started and, more important, why? What was her driving force, if it wasn't fame or fortune?

Krueger-Horn, like Debbi Fields of Mrs. Fields Cookies, had a gift for baking. Both grew up baking cookies. Fields, one of five daughters, made chocolate chip cookies as her contribution to the family. For Krueger-Horn, after years of watching her grandmother cook huge meals on their Ohio farm, cooking was a way of life, an expression of love. It is no surprise that in their early twenties, both women were baking: Fields for her new husband and his co-workers, Krueger-Horn for her entire apartment complex. These acts of creative cooking would become their launching pads to success.

Few of us set out to create multi-million dollar corporations. Most women who think about going into business want to find a way to provide financial security for their families and are concerned with transportation problems or child care or making ends meet from month to month. Many of us look through the classified ads from time to time, just to see what is out there.

There are plenty of opportunities available. The majority of home-based businesses are conducted by women, and millions are successful. Eleven percent of these businesses are reportedly making $54,000 or more, and just over two percent are earning over $120,000 a year.[1] It would seem like few home-based businesses do very well, but remember most them are part-time ventures intended to bring in some extra cash without putting a strain on the family. Because child care and household responsibilities still fall mostly on the shoulders of women and because an increasing number of households in this country are headed by single women, many don't have sufficient time, energy, resources, or freedom from guilt to take on additional jobs outside the home.

Eloise Blackmon of Gary, Indiana, is a good example. Blackmon had a son in kindergarten and a daughter still in diapers. She had trouble keeping a job because of the time she needed to transport her children to day care — her son went to school in the morning and day care in the afternoon. Finding a second job was not an option because the transportation and baby-sitting costs would be more than she could earn. When she wondered aloud if other parents were facing the same difficulty, the answer was a resounding, "You better believe it."

Then, Blackmon hit on an idea. There was a real need for a service she could provide. She borrowed $5,000 from her sister, leased three vans, hired four drivers, set up an additional phone line and radio dispatch center in her basement, and promptly went into business for herself. Within eight months, her monthly revenues were almost $10,000 and her staff and fleet of vans more than doubled. Her company, F&B Transportation, is named after her children — Floyd and Brandy.

The driving factor for starting a business isn't always financial or about child care. For many women it's about change, about wanting something different or better. Jennifer Floren was just twenty-four years old when she stumbled across an idea, or as she puts it, when the light bulb went on. After earning her degree in psychology (with honors) from Dartmouth College, Floren had settled into working with a top management firm in Boston. "It wasn't for me," Floren says. She didn't pin-point what *it* was for her until her younger sister asked to go through her Rolodex file for job leads. That's when Floren realized there was an untapped market for college graduates needing career counseling, from choosing a career field to dressing for an interview. "I began to imagine the possibilities." With only her Rolodex, her telephone, and the help of her Dartmouth alumni, Floren

Jennifer Floren loving what she does

ran Ivy Productions from her home with one goal in mind: to give new professionals personal guidance as they enter the work world.

Floren, Krueger-Horn, Fields, Jenny Craig, and so many others point out time and time again that the basis for a successful business must be passion. Money cannot be the driving factor. There must be an idea, even if it seems wacky.

Something that's fun might be what gets you started. Bobsledding became the stepping stone for my introduction to the business world. It was supposed to be for fun, recreation, exercise, a prove-I-could-do-it kind of a thing. For Linda Katz, it was something she did just for fun that turned into a way of cleaning up those pesky tumbleweeds that blew through her town. One woman's bobsled ride can be another woman's tumbleweed tending.

Cultivating tumbleweeds? Can you do that?

Somewhere on the open Kansas prairie — Garden City, Kansas, to be precise — there roamed an unsuspecting entrepreneur. Linda Katz decided to create a family website, strictly for fun. A recently retired insurance agent, Katz wanted to learn more about websites and decided the best way to learn would be to create her own. "I love the Internet. I'm always on it, looking around."

She bought a book on how to create her own website. Then, she bought a scanner, took some family photos, and went to work setting up a website. "I learned a lot by looking at other people's web pages. So many were really boring: 'This is my dog, and this is my house.' I didn't want to do anything like that."

As a joke she took pictures of her nieces and nephews gathering up tumbleweeds. They wore hard hats (compliments of her husband's construction company) and posed on bull dozers. It was an amusing picture

Linda Katz and family upon their return from harvesting tumbleweeds on the Kansas prairie

for her family. Why would they need hard hats and bull dozers for tumbleweeds? To continue the jest, she named her new website the Prairie Tumbleweed Farm and gave it the motto, "If they don't tumble, we don't sell them."

Claiming the tumbleweeds were organically grown, Katz amused herself even further by listing prices for the novelty items.

Then, it happened. Katz received a phone call. "It was about a week later. I mean, I honestly didn't think anyone other than my own family would see this." But a woman planning a western style wedding saw her home page and wanted a few medium sized tumbleweeds.

"I thought, 'All right, I could help her out. I'll just go outside to my fence here and pick up a few.' I wasn't set up to take credit cards or anything, so I mailed them off to her, and she sent a check. You know, it was kind of fun, but I thought that was the end of it."

It wasn't. Not long after that the producers of the children's show "Barney & Friends" called. Apparently, the purple dinosaur and his little pals were also planning a western theme and wanted a few tumbleweeds to blow through Barney town.

As unbelievable as it seems, this was just the beginning for Katz. She didn't set out to be a businesswoman; she just wanted to have fun. However, Katz would have to learn very quickly about setting up credit card accounts, shipping and handling, and storing her product.

About that same time a thought occurred to Sheli Hanson, a cattle and poultry rancher in central Texas. In the middle of the night Hanson awoke with a great idea: hog's feet. Her farm hands often had to run off wild hogs that roamed her land, leaving behind little piggy prints in the ground. "What if I sold genuine wild hog prints in Texas red clay?" Oven-treated, the clay decorations could come with a history of the Texas wild hogs, could be reasonably priced, and posted on the Internet. Her website? Hogwild!

www.glade.net/~hogwild

Along the bottom of the site's home page, it reads, "No pigs were harmed in this process." Hanson uses only the prints of "free range hogs."

As the title of this book implies, money cannot be the only motivating force in discovering your niche in the business world. You must enjoy what you are doing. You must look forward to a new day, even with its long hours. Katz says, "At no point in my life did I imagine I would be running across the plains, chasing after tumbleweeds, trapping them against fences and saying, 'Oooooh, this looks like a good one.'" But there she is. And what a time she is having.

Cecilia "Pudge" Kleinkauf's motivation was quite different. When in her mid-forties she was diagnosed with skin cancer, she was forced to re-think her life or, as she puts it, reprioritize. "I thought, Oh my God, I'm going to die. So I asked myself what I loved most. Of course, my son came first, but after him, it was flyfishing — being outside with a flyrod in my hand."

Kleinkauf defied the odds by beating cancer and becoming one of a very few female flyfishing instructors in the country. She created her own business from a life she thought was lost. Sixteen years later, there's still excitement in her voice when she speaks about flyfishing. There is

Kleinkauf and fellow flyfisher on Montague Island, Alaska, with a bright Coho salmon

also an intensity that tells you her business was bound to be a success. "I just kept my eye on the target [enjoying flyfishing]. I just want to get other women to do it because it is so wonderful."

Perhaps you have an idea already in mind. Whether it's flyfishing or catching tumbleweeds, the idea must be yours. As Fields says, "You can't motivate another person to come up with an idea, to invent something. It is something inherently in you."

Most people have a talent that is uniquely theirs. Fields' talent is creating and baking cookies. When she first married, she was the typical 1970s happy homemaker, but that persona quickly faded. "I would go to business parties with my husband, and I would see people's eyes glaze over when they asked what I did for a living." Being a housewife suddenly lost its novelty. To make herself feel better, she baked cookies and sent them to business meetings with her husband. She experienced tremendous satisfaction as the cookies were quickly gobbled up.

No one specifically walked up to Fields and suggested she sell the cookies. It was just a feeling that came to her. She had seen how people behaved when they ate her cookies: they loved them. Fields became known as the cookie maker, and people were visibly disappointed if her husband showed up empty-handed at a meeting.

Like Krueger-Horn, Fields' cookies became an extension of herself, something she wanted to share with other people. Jenny Craig's business also became a way of helping other women, so they could feel as vivacious and healthy as she did. Anyone who has been overweight and succeeded in shedding those extra pounds knows the resulting feeling of freedom and burst of energy and wants to share them with others. Craig is no exception. Then again, maybe she is. Rather than just talk about it, she sprang into action.

Craig gained — and held onto — more than forty-five pounds after a difficult pregnancy. Her mother was overweight, also, before she died of an obesity-related stroke. All Craig could think about was that she wanted to live to see her daughters fully grown. Determined to get fit, she joined a gym and changed her life forever. Her story goes on from there, but the point is clear: as passion took hold, so did her successes.

Jennifer Maxwell's top priority was graduating from the University of California at Berkeley with a degree in nutrition and food science. She was just twenty years old and not entirely sure of what she wanted to do with herself. Her interests, sports and nutrition, became motivating factors for an idea that would be wildly successful.

As a cross-country runner, finding a healthy, energy-boosting snack that could sustain her — and other athletes — throughout long runs became a mission, a passion. Using her lab classes as the test kitchen for her idea, Maxwell began the search for the perfect energy bar. The result was PowerBar.

Now grossing more than $150 million in sales, PowerBar dominates the energy bar market. Maxwell did not set out to create an empire. She just wanted something that could sustain her energy for a good, long run. She followed her passion.

Jennifer Maxwell's love of sports and interest in nutrition came together in the creation of PowerBar

Whether you are going to start a business purely for the joy of self-expression, to support a lifestyle, or to fulfill a dream, as long as you have the determination and passion, you have the means. You will discover several creative, nontraditional, and down-right daring ways women have changed the rules to make their dreams come true.

There are plenty of opportunities to start a home-based business; however, the question, for many, is *what*: What can I do? The answer lies with you. Since my interview with Linda Katz, my husband continues to suggest I set up a website offering to sell fertilizer — we have two eighty-pound dogs living in the house with us. Personally, I would love the idea of selling organically grown, ahem, fertilizer, but I see shipping and handling as more of a problem than I care to take on.

Fantasize About Your Future

No matter how crazy the idea, don't abandon it. Who would have thought Jenai Lane could put a bathtub stopper and chain around her neck, call it a necklace, and start a successful business? But she did. Aiming her hip-hop sense of style toward Generation X consumers, Lane went from struggling college student to jewelry and cosmetic magnate. Her company, Respect, Inc., became a $1 million-per-year novelty item corporation in three years and one of the fifty fastest growing small businesses in the United States.

Floren also took only three years to turn an idea into a successful, well-polished networking machine. Her Boston-based Ivy Productions even publishes a magazine that has several thousand subscribers. In a publication partnership with *Forbes* magazines, *experience* magazine is the only business publication for twenty-somethings and is pulling in more than $2 million in revenue.

Katz's Prairie Tumbleweed Farm gets phone calls from around the world requesting tumbleweeds — even tumbleweed Christmas trees. Movie producers, entertainment industry buyers, and party organizers call her with rush orders. Who would have thought? "Our website has been getting as many as 400 hits a day. In fact, just today, my husband and I boxed up twenty tumbleweeds to ship out." And the orders keep coming in.

Ideas can come to you as a necessity or as some crazy whim that is just wacky enough to work. If you like it, if it makes you feel good, you've taken the first good steps. Stay with it.

Traditionally, massage therapists only worked from their homes or traveled to their clients homes. So when Diane Slater and Helen Yee decided to open their own massage therapy school, they were moving into unchartered territory. Never before had there been a massage therapy clinic in the state of Ohio. In fact, Slater and Yee succeeded in creating a school in the only state where massage therapy is regulated by the state's medical board. "It was tough going, but we qualified, set up the program and signed our first lease," says

Slater and Yee conduct hands on massage classes

Slater. From there, both their dreams and the school keep expanding. They found a need and filled it.

Kristin Penta always fantasized about creating her own cosmetic line. Concocting different potions on her mother's stove, Penta wanted to be the next Estee Lauder. But when it came time to chose her college and major, "My father said, 'There's no way you're going to major in lip gloss.'" Penta humored her parents, graduating from Clark University with double degrees, psychology and business. But the love of cosmetics never went away.

Penta applied for jobs at Estee Lauder, Avon, and Revlon, only to discover that the actual product was not created on site, but at an off-site science laboratory or manufacturing plant. It was then that her entrepreneurial spirit was awakened. Penta wanted to be part of the actual concocting, pouring, and stirring of the product. So she put her business degree to work and created Fun Cosmetics. Penta may have majored in business, but she certainly graduated to lip gloss — and a company with a projected revenue of $5 million.

Most women have a need to express creative ideas, share their visions with friends and community, and make a positive difference in the world.

Some of the products and services mentioned in this chapter are completely new or unique concepts — wild and crazy ideas just wacky enough to appeal to today's consumers. Bathroom stoppers as necklaces and tumbleweed Christmas trees are completely original ideas, but that doesn't mean you have to think as creatively or abstractly. Some of the ideas and products are extensions or modifications of already existing products: a better chocolate chip cookie, a hipper career counseling service. Find your passion and ask yourself, How can I make this better?

Now, Take the Next Step

The problem is, no matter how great the idea, most of us tend to stall. We question ourselves. Is the idea really that great? Can it work? Women, in particular, do this. If it is a really good idea, often we figure someone will step in and help us — rescue us. The idea of going it alone is a frightening one, and without realizing it, we often sabotage ourselves. While we all say we want success, often women tend to avoid it. Few of us have been socialized to expect or demand it. We say it can't be done because of our family. We can't because of our children. We have no time. We have no resources. Our friends won't like it, or people will laugh at us.

Consider this scenario. Restless in my new role as an at-home mother, I fantasized about something new and exciting. Then I heard the U.S. Bobsled Federation was looking for women for the first U.S. women's bobsled team. I've always been spontaneous, so immediately I sent in my athletic résumé. Now, let's get serious. As a twenty-eight-year-old and a new mother of a six-month-old baby girl, there was no way they'd ever consider someone like me. Right?

Imagine my surprise when I received a phone call inviting me to the Olympic Training Center in Lake Placid, New York, for a week-long

The 1996 U.S. women's bobsled team at Lake Placid, New York

camp. Within days, I received the official packet in the mail, including a long list of items I would need: shoulder pads, knee pads, duck tape, helmet, goggles, weight-lifting belt to protect the kidneys, and rib pads.

Good Lord! What have I gotten myself into? I was still twenty pounds overweight, nursing my little girl, and out of shape. I was terrified, but this was an opportunity of a lifetime. I had to go. If I didn't, I knew I would wonder for the rest of my life. So I hired a personal trainer and got to work.

We really didn't have the money for the flight to Lake Placid, yet my family found a way for me to go. My mother, sister, and husband were my baby-sitters and biggest supporters as I flew off on this adventure. When I got there, I was sure everyone was asking: What is she doing here? Who is she kidding? I was afraid people were laughing at me. I was afraid of what my friends thought.

By the end of the week, I was battered, bruised, and sore, but I was invited to come back. Seven months later, after grueling training, a tailored diet, and more determination than I've ever felt in my life, I returned to win the gold medal in the first national competition for women bobsledders. I was a bobber! I was able to do it because I overcame my fear of trying and possibly failing. Fields did the same and look at her now. "I wonder how many people have been thinking of something for years but have been afraid to try," she ponders.

Terry Neece, former president of the National Association of Women Business Owners, concurs. Because something appears to be too difficult, too out of reach, too wild, she says, we give up. "We strangle entrepreneurship." Whether it's jumping into a bobsled or taking on a new concept, the only way to make it happen is to move. "I am a fond believer in whatever the mind can conceive, you can achieve," Neece says.

There are two myths that can strangle our initiative and our ideas if we listen to them:

• If I try my hand at my own business, I risk losing all my money.

• Women in general are lousy risk-takers.

The first myth is disproved by cold hard data. IDC/Link, a New York research firm that tracks the small office/home office (SOHO) market, reports full-time, home-based business owners have incomes twenty percent higher than households in general. And the majority of these home-based entrepreneurs are women. Sarah Edwards, co-author of *The Best Home Businesses for the 90s*, says it is not at all uncommon for home-based businesses to earn six- or seven-figure salaries.[2]

What about the second myth? It is more difficult for women to be risk-takers, right? I mean, that's what the experts tell us, isn't it? That view is not mirrored in today's realities, however. The majority of women who start new businesses capitalize their own ventures and choose businesses completely unrelated to their previous work experience. These factors indicate most female entrepreneurs are indeed taking considerable risks.

Krueger-Horn was working for a major sportswear outlet in New York City and flying home on weekends to Ohio to start a cookie business. Lynette Reed, an unemployed model, saw the potential for a candle shop in Los Angeles. She sold all her personal belongings — including her television, jewelry, and furniture — for the money to rent a space and open a candle store.

Jacquelyn Hughes Mooney drove taxi cabs in New Orleans and provided child care. Sewing decorative pillows was only a hobby until 1994 when she decided to chuck her other jobs and sell her pillows full-time. The pillows quickly sold out at craft shows, and she turned her hand to quilting. This former cab driver now has clients such as Oprah Winfrey, Bryant Gumbel, Gladys Knight, and Maya Angelou.

Gretchen Leddy worked as a keypunch operator at a small savings and loan in Cleveland, Ohio. Miserable with the long hours and her surroundings, Leddy joked with a friend who was a business broker. "I asked him, 'You got any bakeries for sale?'" Leddy had taken a cake decorating class for fun and had fallen in love. In addition to appeasing her sweet tooth, baking was a source of comfort for her. Sometime later, to the surprise of both Gretchen and her husband, Bernie, the Leddys got a phone call from their friend. There was, in fact, a bakery for sale — in Columbus, Ohio.

"I just thought, 'Can we do this?' I had mixed emotions. It happened so quickly. But this was my idea. This was something I wanted. It was my dream and Bernie just said, 'Okay. Let's do it.'" Now she owns and operates Bachman's Bakery.

Diane Jacobs, cake artist and owner of The Cakeworks in Los Angeles, initially studied architecture at the University of Cincinnati, but had always loved baking. Talk about owning a vision. When Jacobs was twenty-one years old, she saw beautiful cakes featured on a television show. Immediately, she wrote the owner of the shop and asked about job opportunities. Upon his response, Jacobs packed her bags and moved to Los Angeles to live out her dreams.

Finally, Ruth Fertel was a divorced mother of two with a degree in chemistry and physics in 1965 when she risked it all by mortgaging her home to buy a steakhouse. Now, seventy years old, Fertel presides over fifty-nine steakhouses nationwide and runs a corporation that netted $176 million in 1997.

All these women were proactive. They took chances. They took the necessary steps to follow their dreams. They followed their passions. Once you've discovered your passion — what it is you want to share or need to do — you must do the same. Although the ideas came easily enough, believing you can turn your idea or dream into a reality can be more difficult. To do that you must avoid two major pitfalls: procrastination and second-guessing yourself.

According to the Women's Business Enterprise National Council's executive director Susan Bari, being proactive is extremely important to your success. Psychologists have found that procrastination is a common plague, particularly among women. Women business leaders tend to be perfectionists. The fear of not being perfect, of letting down friends, family, and co-workers may cause them to stall. This fear is also the reason women are more likely to pull all-nighters and create an environment in which they are completely consumed with a specific project. They must own every last detail. And while many women feel like they work best under pressure, experts all agree it is not the way to go into business.

Admittedly, it is difficult to break free of this trait. But ask any of today's top executives, it becomes essential for your health and the vitality of your business. Ask the woman who created necklaces from bathtub stoppers and made millions from it, or talk to the women who were once making less than $20,000 a year and now have celebrities like Goldie Hawn, Melanie Griffith, Oprah Winfrey, and Rosie O'Donnell as clients. They will tell you spontaneity and faith in yourself are keys, but you must be organized. While all of these women took huge risks in the beginning of their projects, they have learned to approach their businesses in a calm, organized, methodical manner to avoid unnecessary mistakes. Almost all have said that if they had known what a feasibility study was and if they had done one, perhaps the number and kind of mistakes they made would have been less problematic.

Trust Your Instincts

Second-guessing yourself is easy enough to do, as well. You certainly don't need any help from others in that department: lots of people will be only too happy to give you all kinds of free advice. Just keep in mind this rule of thumb: you get what you pay for. As quickly as all the business and financial advisers were gobbling down Fields' cookies, they were telling her that her cookie business would never succeed. Reed heard over and over that she would never be able to obtain a small business loan for her candle shop. This is when you must decide what you think, how much you believe in yourself, and what you are willing to risk for your dream to become a reality.

In 1963, Mary Kay Ash of Mary Kay Cosmetics retired from a successful career in sales. Restless, Ash decided to write a book to help women get ahead in the male-dominated business world. She made two lists: all the positive things she'd learned and experienced from her previous job and all the areas that needed improvement. But as she reviewed the lists, she realized that she had created the perfect marketing plan for her own business.

Initially, her plan was to write a self-help business book for women. Instead, by applying her knowledge as a salesperson — specifically a female salesperson — to her love of cosmetics, Ash created the best-selling brand of facial, skin, and color cosmetics and the largest direct seller of skin care products in the United States. But, her beginning was quite modest. Taking $5,000 from her personal savings, Ash and her twenty-year-old son launched Mary Kay Cosmetics in late 1963 from her home in Dallas, Texas. Ash's knowledge of the market, the direct sales system, and her customers (women) brought her tremendous success.

Women know more than they think they do. They just need to learn to listen to themselves. Dr. Anne Moir, Ph.D., and David Jessel found that women have greater accuracy in their initial gut reactions than men do. In their book, *Brain Sex: The Real Difference Between Men & Women*, they reaffirm what women have suspected for years: because women have better listening and communication skills, their senses are more highly developed and acute. Period. These include intuition. Unfortunately, however, most women tend to second-guess themselves.

As Neece reminds us, "If you have a vision or a dream, you have to move to make it happen. No matter how crazy it is. Think of all the crazy and elaborate ideas, write them down, and really look at them. Whatever you believe, it will happen."

If you can conceive, you can achieve.

Second-guessing is a natural reaction. Women do it to protect themselves, but sometimes, unconsciously, they do it to sabotage themselves.

Answer the Fundamental Questions

There are several questions you need to ask yourself. This is first.

What do I have to lose by going forward with my dream?

Blackmon and Reed sold what they owned and borrowed money from family. Fields and her husband put a lean on their mortgage. Krueger-Horn continued to hold her job in New York, flying home on the weekends to meet with her business partner and putting all the expenditures on credit cards. Leddy and Mooney quit their jobs, giving up secure paychecks. Mary Kay Ash risked her life savings. The roads to all of these women's dreams were, undoubtedly, risky. Yet their risks paid off.

Perhaps you are ready to take a risk. You have an idea; you've found your passion. You're not procrastinating, and you're not second-guessing yourself. Now you need a plan.

Joy Mangano swore to herself she would never lose out on an idea again; so when she came up with the Miracle Mop idea, she knew she had to act. Mangano saw an existing product that could use improvement. "I was mopping when I thought of it. I thought, 'I need to invent a better way to do this.' My back was hurting, and my hands hurt. It should be the last mop that anyone ever buys."

Mangano went straight to work. She laid out her ideas. It must be a metal that never rusts. Wood rots over time. You shouldn't have to bend over, touch the dirty water, or dry out your hands from the chlorine detergent. "I put it all on paper and took it to someone to design the product. You don't have to be an engineer." For Mangano, she collected enough money to pay someone to create her prototype. It was, she believes, her first wise investment in the business world.

Taking that first step is the toughest. You have fantasized about your idea for sometime. Perhaps, you've mustered enough nerve to talk about it with family and friends. You believe in yourself and your idea. Your best sense — intuition — tells you to go on. Now what?

You need to do a business plan or at least a feasibility study and report. But how do you do them? If the idea is an actual product, describing it on paper, as Mangano did, is the first step. However, as Krueger-Horn and Ash can attest, a business plan is about more than cookies or lipstick. You are creating a business. Just as Ash sat down at her kitchen table to create her marketing list, you must also write out your intentions. Answer the following questions for yourself:

- What is it that I want?
- How will I do this?
- Where do I envision this dream taking me?
- How will I make it feasible?

You Must Do Your Homework

You can learn from Annalisa Mastroianni. She left her job as a waitress to start her own catering business, providing nutritionally individualized meals to clients' doorsteps. Her approach to caring for the nutritional needs of her clients is ideal for people on the go, and it caught on. Annie's Edibles was a hit, but Mastroianni had not taken time to create her business on paper. In truth, there was too little time. Things moved too quickly. What she hadn't thought about was what she really needed to know to become a personal chef and caterer. "I loved to cook, and I was the best damned waitress you ever had. I could tell you what you ordered from me ten years ago."

But as Annie's Edibles grew, along with her celebrity clientele, having good people skills and knowing her way around the kitchen wasn't enough. "Now, I understand the importance of a business plan. I needed to know how much insurance I should have and how much it was going to cost me. I should have been aware of the seasonal changes in this business, the price of beef, and an appropriate amount to spend on marketing. I should have known [more] about how much rent against how many clients I needed to cover costs …. I wish I would have put more effort into [learning] that in the beginning. I could have saved myself a lot of trouble."

Mastroianni learned the hard way how to effectively and successfully run a business. As she laughingly described it in retrospect, she was "up a creek without a paddle."

By drawing on the experience of all the great businesswomen discussed in these pages, perhaps you can chart a straighter course. You can profit from the lessons cookie-magnate Debbi Fields learned the hard way about being a risk-taker and marketing herself.

There are several things you can do to reduce your risks and improve your path to success. The key activities you will learn about are:

- Writing a clear, concise mission statement,
- Creating a feasibility study,
- Researching your product or service and your proposed business, and
- Developing a business plan.

By knowing yourself, what resources you have available, and as much as possible about the business you are proposing to start, you can cast off assured of a smoother ride with both paddles securely in the water.

Chapter 2

Why Am I Doing This?

⸺

In our sports book, *The Quiet Storm: A Celebration of Women in Sport*, co-author Michelle Powe and I ask the question, "Why am I doing this?" It is a question that all athletes ask themselves from time to time, and it is a question that businesspeople must also ask themselves. It is also one of the first things a career counselor will ask you: What is it that you want? What are you expecting?

Gretchen Leddy had complained of the long hours she put in as a keypunch operator in Cleveland; yet, with her new business, the hours are just as long. The difference, of course, is they are hours that belong to her. They are her baker hours. "Bernie and I didn't want to work for other people. It has always been a dream of ours [to have a business of our own]. I wanted to work for myself. Now, the only people I have to answer to are my customers, by pleasing them. That's perfect."

You may have been thinking of going into business for years and years, or perhaps this is a new notion, something fresh and exciting. Whatever your reasons for deciding to start your own business, they are personal ones. You may want an added income or more hours to spend with your family. You may need to see an idea become reality. Whatever the reason, your internal choices, influenced by external pressures, will determine your decision to carry on or quit.

If you are researching your idea or looking for added inspiration because you've decided to forge ahead with your dream, it is a good time to consider the advice given universally by business experts: don't be foolish. While all agree being a risk-taker is imperative to success, no one said anything about rushing in unprepared. Risk-taking is not synonymous with foolhardiness.

When Cozy Wolan, creator of Cozy's Cuts for Kids, decided to change professions and open her own children's hair salon, she didn't step blindly into a new, unchartered world. In fact, she says it took her two and one-half years from the time she came up with the concept until the time she actually opened her doors for business.

Unlike so many other people — present company included — she did not simply sit around tossing out ideas. Wolan immediately went into action. No, she didn't quit her job. She began her research.

The idea came to her when a friend took her nephew to get his hair cut at a typical hair salon. He cried so much, both her friend and the nephew were asked to leave the salon. The more Wolan thought about a hair salon just for children, the more she liked it.

Why weren't there hair salons that were kid-friendly — places with toys and games and other things that would distract the children and make them want to come back again and again?

"I got excited thinking about the possibilities," Wolan says. "I would think, Why don't they do this or this? That line of thinking quickly evolved to, I would have a cappuccino bar for the mothers, and I would have toys for the kids.

"It actually took me six months to leave my job," Wolan laughs now. That was when the real research began. Armed with the idea of what she wanted, Wolan took a job as a store clerk at a toy store and served as manager of an indoor playground in New York. She studied the market. "I really, really did my homework and learned what they [consumers] were looking for."

Then the final touch: Wolan earned her license in hairdressing.

Wolan believes that sheer determination, belief in her product, and research, research, research got her where she is today. Now with two locations in Manhattan, Cozy's clientele includes children of such celebrities as Rosie O'Donnell, Isabella Rossellini, Meg Ryan and Dennis Quad, Pierce Brosnan and Keely Shaye Smith, Natasha Richardson and

Liam Neeson, Donna Dixon and Dan Aykroyd, Phoebe Cates and Kevin Kline, Kevin Bacon and Kyra Sedgwick, Wayne Gretzky and Janet Jones, Sigourney Weaver, and Ricki Lake, to name several. Actress Natasha Richardson says of Cozy's Cuts for Kids, "After you've been there, you wouldn't dream of sending your kids to a normal hairdresser."[1] Wow, talk about a marketing dream.

Cozy Wolan, husband Joe Friedman, Shane, and Riley

Still, with all the research, Wolan admits it was a frightening time. "Because you are starting a new concept, it's very scary." Certainly, Wolan was a risk-taker, but she was also practical about it, doing a lot of research before investing any real money into the project. In *Why Good Girls Don't Get Ahead ... But Gutsy Girls Do*, author Kate White suggests that being gutsy means going with your instinct, going after what you want, and not worrying what others think of the idea — a concept by which we all operated when we were very young.[2]

I was particularly interested in the point about gutsy girls. In *The Quiet Storm*, Powe and I theorized that it is the tomboy mentality that drives successful women. We were not at all surprised to learn that more than eighty percent of the women in the top *Fortune* 500 were self-described tomboys.[3] Risk-takers. Dare-devils. The kids who parachuted off the backyard shed. After adolescence, most girls go through several changes as they learn how to act like ladies, be polite, mind their Ps and Qs, and cross their Ts. These successful women did not unlearn their early lessons with the backyard shed. They are successful today because they retain that competitive spirit so prevalent in sports-loving men. Not the popular, "I must win," but the ever powerful, "Yes, I can."

Wolan does not refer to herself as a tomboy, but says she has great determination. "One of the things my vendors always tell me is that I can get anything I want. And anything that I want, I can get. Because I am very determined, and I do not ever take *no* for an answer." Sports or no sports, Wolan possesses that "I can" perspective.

Case in point. When Wolan first opened her shop, she needed to order a moderate supply of specific items to run the salon. Hers was a small hair salon with a very limited budget. What she found, however, was that the supply companies had an order minimum. "My vendors would come back to me and say, 'Sorry, Cozy, they won't take your order.' And I would say, 'Well, give me the number of so-and-so, and I'll call them.' They would just say, 'Uh oh, look out.'"

Tomboy or no, that is the kind of sports-minded thinking that kept Betty Harrigan's book, *Games Mother Never Taught You,* on the best seller lists for months and months. The year was 1977, and Harrigan's thinking was a bit militant. She advised women to use sports analogies to get ahead and do whatever it took to win, which included crushing the opponent and burning bridges. However, the traditional negative connotation attached to women being competitive left many women feeling very uncomfortable with that new plan of attack. In addition, some of the most competitive people I know are women, women are by nature team players. Fortunately, in the business world, this is a good thing. Selling your idea at all costs is not. Being a team player will ultimately be part of your big payoff.

Debbi Fields of Mrs. Fields Cookies describes the competitive spirit perfectly: "Sports are like business — they are fun. Nobody ever starts a game with the idea of losing. Yet in the end, when you do lose a game, the most important aspect is the sense of camaraderie. That is essential. It helps you maintain good sportsmanship. You may end the game losing, but you walk away with a greater conviction for winning next time. Also, you want to win *with* your teammates, so you're never really a loser."

In other words, you took a risk. You tried. The payoff was a lesson learned. There is always a payoff. Every business woman I spoke to insisted that with every failed attempt or calamity came a lesson. It is okay to try, then fail, as long as you try again. Sports teach us that. Sports provide other useful guidelines, as well.

"I also love that they [sports] have clearly defined rules," Fields says. "Everyone knows what the penalty box looks like and that you foul out when you step out of bounds. But, in life, we don't communicate all the rules when we are talking about business. I like to think about what the rules are here. How can we win without being fouled out? What do I need to communicate to people so they will understand the penalties and rules? How could I have better prepared myself for the game?"

Research, Research, Research

Diving into a business venture without proper research is very much like diving into a bobsled for the first time. You are completely unprepared for the disasters to come. When the U.S. women first took to the slopes, no one bothered to tell us what to do in the event of a crash. The ride itself was terrifying enough. Zipping along the mile-long track at eighty miles per hour, we felt completely out of control.

> My God! Why am I doing this? What am I doing here? Am I really ready for this?

We just kept our heads down, crossed our fingers, and hoped we would cross the finish line safely.

The first time I crashed, as insane as this sounds, I had no idea what was happening. The ride is so loud, frightening, and rough anyway, when my driver flipped our sled over, it took a couple of seconds for me to realize we had capsized. Suddenly, I truly was hanging on for dear life. I could feel gravity pulling me out of the sled, prying my fingers off of my side handlebars — the only thing keeping me in the sled. I had not been taught the rules. I did not know how to position my head and shoulders to help fight the gravity. I did not know how to keep my body from getting ice burn.

Eventually, gravity won. I was ejected from the sled, free falling, with a real risk of the sled rolling on top of me, crushing me. That next few seconds while the 500-pound sled and I sped along on our sides on the ice were terrifying. Then, we parted ways.

When I got down the mountain, the first thing I did was pull a Canadian slider to the side and ask how I could have done things differently. I learned my lesson and wished mightily that I had known better before. I licked my wounds later with several ice packs and the resolve never to do that again.

This experience was similar to those of many businesswomen. While they are not nearly crushed by a speeding bobsled, many have been devastated financially. Most have known the terror of the unknown and the uncertainty of whether they could finish the race.

There are much safer ways to find out about the game. Take Tara Cronbaugh, for example. She knew, once she had her great idea for being in the coffeehouse business, she needed to find out more. Instead of flying by the seat of her pants, the twenty-year-old University of Iowa sophomore began a two-year research project. This included subscribing to and pouring over all the trade magazines, becoming a member of such organizations as the Specialty Coffee Association of America, and networking with other coffee shop owners, managers, and vendors. Despite the fact she didn't even like coffee before all this, Cronbaugh began her quest to develop a taste for all the coffee blends. She even taught herself to discern from what origins the blends were created. There is more, but you get the idea. Her notion was, "How could I expect to sell something I didn't even understand?"

Flyfishing didn't just come to "Pudge" Kleinkauf in the middle of night. She'd flyfished for a couple of years. It was a relaxing, recreational sport, and nothing made her happier than having a flyrod in her hand. When she was diagnosed with cancer, she turned to this sport for comfort. Still working at the University of Alaska at Anchorage's department of social work, she became a part-time flyfishing instructor. After all, learning the sport and business from the inside, first, was the best experience. By the time Kleinkauf dedicated herself fully to the profession of flyfishing, she could tell you the differences between all the different flyrods and waders on the market.

Whether it is a product or a concept you are working on, be sure you understand what you are stepping into. As Fields suggests, understanding the rules and penalties is the safest route for any aspiring athlete or businessperson. Below are some general rules these successful, self-made businesswomen followed.

Gather Information

Find out if your idea is really a new idea or, perish the thought, if your service or product is already available to the public. The chocolate chip cookie was not exactly new. Before Mrs. Fields

Cookies, there was a wide variety of cookies, but with a commonality: they were crisp. What was new, however, was the soft, chewy cookie. Krueger-Horn found there were no other gourmet shops offering dessert items. While Mrs. Fields Cookies was well established by then, Krueger-Horn was able to put a new spin on things by opening a gourmet cookie and dessert shop. Headhunter companies already existed, but Floren discovered that none were exclusively dedicated to twenty-something professionals.

When B. Smith was asked if there was 'room for her' in the Martha Stewart market, she offered this philosophy: "Coke never put Pepsi out of business. Burger King hasn't put McDonald's out of business. There's room for both of us."

Smith researched the home decorations market and found that, indeed, there was room. As she says, the 90s have become a nesting period for most Americans. Baby boomers are becoming more home-oriented, building memories and traditions for the family, and looking for ways to create their own sense of style. Enter *B. Smith With Style*, her magazine.[4]

Write Down Your Idea

Once you know your idea is unique and has the potential for success, write down your idea on a simple piece of paper. Date it, take it to a notary public, then file it away. This may be an unnecessary step, but for your own assurance, do it anyway. Then, prepare a nondisclosure document — discussed later — and make copies you can have with you when you talk with others. These precautions protect your idea from others stealing or copying it. You can obtain more information from the following sources:

• Commissioner of Patents, Washington, D.C. 20231

• U.S. Copyright Office, Washington, D.C. 20559

• *Develop and Market Your Creative Ideas,* by Dale A. Davis

Talk to Business People

When Jennifer Floren realized she wanted to open a career counseling business, she talked to other business owners around her. She familiarized herself with the headhunting business and the how-tos of creating dynamite résumés. When she did so, she was careful not to say exactly what she had in mind for her new business, Ivy Productions. Joy Mangano was equally cautious not to let her competition — the very people she was seeking advice from — know too much about what she was creating when she devised the Miracle Mop.

Remember, asking for opinions in the business world can be as tricky as inventors sharing ideas with each other. Not all advice is good. Not everyone is fair. Ideas can be stolen. It is important to find the right people to ask. A good first step is to call the relevant business organizations that are listed in the Resources section.

Talk with everyone in the business community. Ask each one, "What would you do if you were me?" After you have done this, plot out your next action steps.

Get Involved

"Business owners, especially women, need to get involved in politics because every political decision can affect your bottom line." Terry Neece, owner of Terry Neece Personnel Services and President of GrassRoots Impact, a corporate and political strategy firm, frequently testifies in Congress on small business issues. But there was a time when she was Terry Neece, an up-and-coming owner of her own personnel service business, naïve about local politics. Having just bought her very own office building, she was on Cloud Nine. She had great hopes of expanding quickly. Instead, she got a hard lesson in politics.

As soon as she moved into her building, a construction company

(L to R) NFIB representative; Congressman Jim Talent (R. MO); Terry Neese; Congressman Harris Fawell (R-IL, retired); Congresswoman Sue Kelly (R-NY)

began tearing up the highway that provided the sole access to her building. For nearly three years, customers and employees were forced to park three or more blocks away and put up with the inconveniences caused by the construction. Who knows how many possible clients she lost?

"I didn't listen to the news or read the paper because I was so focused on growing my business. If I had, I would have been aware of the upcoming highway closure when I bought the building."

Write Out a First Draft of Your Mission Statement

Earlier, you asked yourself questions about what you want. Now you need to go a step further and develop your mission statement. Just as you would write a proposal or cover letter for work, write out what it is you want and what you want to do. Describe:

• What your intentions are
• What it is that you want
• What your resources are
• What you have gleaned from the people you've talked with
• What your assets are
• What ways you might get the wheels of your idea in motion

Before Jenny Craig and her husband, Sid, could or would do anything, she recalls, "We had to see it on paper." She wanted to create a personalized weight loss program, and writing a mission statement was a way they could clarify their goals and have a guide to keep them on target. As a seasoned professional, Craig knew it was imperative to write out her goals in the form of a mission statement. By doing so, both Jenny and Sid had a guide to use for forming their business and staying focused on their true goals.

I knew I loved to bobsled. I knew I wanted women bobsledders in the Olympics. What else was there to know? As we faced the International Olympic Committee and prospects of gaining corporate sponsorship, we had to create a mission statement. It's funny how our relationships changed — even to the sport of bobsledding — when we were challenged by creating a mission statement for the U.S. women's bobsled team. Money, budgets, deadlines, and quotas can take the zip-a-dee-doo-da out of just about anything unless you have passion for all aspects of attaining the goal. Creating a mission statement is hard work. It requires research and honesty and is vital to success. Ironically, three of the women who helped create the mission statement did not return the following year. There is always a chance, you might discover from your own mission statement, either you don't really want to do it after all or you want to modify your goals. It's better to find out now, rather than later when you could be in too deep to get out without major losses.

Secure Your Own Future

You've done the research. You're sure you've stumbled onto something unique. You have a quality product or service to offer. But it is important you don't let your dreams run away with you, or vise versa. Again, it is important to ask yourself what the ramifications of this risk-taking venture can be. Will you still be happy with this decision five years from now? Remember, seven out of every ten new businesses fail each year. Perhaps those would-be entrepreneurs did not research and plan, write mission statements, or do feasibility reports. You must determine, what makes your business idea so special? How can you assure its success, and how could it fail?

Fields asked herself these questions again and again, as did Krueger-Horn. Fields did the research. She knew there were no chewy, oversized chocolate chip cookies on the market, and she knew they would be extremely popular. Time and time again she was told by the *experts* that her plan would never work, but her instinct told her the experts were wrong. She listened to her instincts and went on to run a multi-million dollar corporation. However, she took a significant risk.

As we will see later, Krueger-Horn knew that her product idea was original. She knew that she had stumbled onto an untapped and, she believed, unserved market, but she was taking a big chance.

The element of risk is always there in business. It is part of the challenge, and it must always be taken into account in your thinking and planning. You can minimize the amount of risk involved through good research.

An example of the importance of research before action comes from my own experiences in the literary world. I know many authors who, frustrated by the highly competitive field of publishing, turn to self-publication as a way of sharing their work. The cost is usually between $8,000 to $10,000, usually requiring a loan from a bank or family member. Authors who have taken this route hope they can sell enough books to break even. Since most authors fall into the starving artist category, breaking even is a success. Getting published is a miracle.

As you might suspect, authors are not necessarily very good business people, and many do not realize that the only way to sell is to have a strong marketing plan. Despite the promises of self-publication houses, they do not promote an author's books.

One struggling author of childrens' books thought she had done all the research about self-publishing. After an initial investment of eight grand for book development, self-publishing seemed like a great solution since she was ready and willing to invest the time to promote herself. Unfortunately, what she did not know was that newspapers, television, radio, and magazine book critics have a standing policy not to review self-published works. However, no one at the self-publishing house told her this. How could she possibly promote her work?

Now 500 copies of her book lay collecting dust in a warehouse. What she should have done, before diving into self-publishing, was talk to other self-published authors, talk to newspaper and magazine critics, and more carefully weigh her options. If she had performed her own feasibility study, she would have seen that the risk of taking out a loan from her bank was impractical.

It is hard to overstate the importance of doing research, of knowing all the rules of the game before you start to play.

Location, Location, Location

Another important consideration is where you should locate your business. Where is the best place for the kind of facility your business requires? Location of your business is an important part of your marketing strategy. If you can't bring people to the product or the product to the people, you'll lose the game before you begin.

Remember Lynette Reed, the unemployed model who sold all her life belongings to start a candle shop? Finding the perfect location was what made her success. Using all her savings and lifelong belongings, Reed raised $12,000 to cover start-up costs and rented a space in a very chic neighborhood in Los Angeles. What sold her was that the neighborhood was frequented by a coffee shop clientele willing to pay $5 for a latté. Reed reasoned that this same group of people just might be willing to buy candles for $20.

It was a risk that paid off when, at Christmas, actress Melanie Griffith ordered 120 gift baskets for her closest friends and associates in the entertainment industry. The gifts were a hit, and word of Reed's shop spread quickly. Today, she <u>employs</u> more than seventy full-time employees and has contracts with Nordstrom, Macy's, The Nature Co., the Discovery Channel, and Lazarus for her scented candles. Her gross sales skyrocketed 1,000 percent, from $300,000 in 1996 to an estimated $3,000,000 in 1998.

In Ray Kroc's book, *Grinding It Out*, the founder of McDonald's details how he would use a helicopter to fly over cities and see where schools, churches, playgrounds, and certain traffic patterns were to find the ideal location for a new store. Kroc understood his market and the importance of location for a store to be success.

Diane Jacobs, owner of The Cakeworks, Inc. in Los Angeles, had an accountant who thought she should get a warehouse in East Los Angeles because the location she had chosen in the city was too expensive. "Yet, I was always told the first thing to consider was location, location, location. I knew no one was going to come to East L.A. to buy a cake."

Instead, Jacobs put her store in the fashionable La Brea area of Los Angeles Her clients include celebrities such as Roseanne, Kevin Kline, Jim Carrey, Tyra Banks, Halle Berry, Steven Spielberg, Quincy Jones, Julia Roberts, Jennifer Tilly, and Nora Dunn. Jacobs designed the cake for the 100th episode celebration for the cast of "Party Of Five", and has provided the cakes for many other shows' parties: "General Hospital," "Melrose Place," and "Beverly Hills 90210," to drop several names.

Diane Jacob's cake for the 100th episode of the "Party of Five"

Tess Rano and local school teachers send a greeting during a workout in one of her kickboxing classes

Location is everything for Tess Rano's karate and kickboxing school. She located the Ernie Reyes School of Karate within two miles of three different public school districts. The kickboxing classes have become a great outlet for the nearby elementary school teachers.

For Tara Cronbaugh, the success of a coffee house had everything to do with books. Even before the whole "Friends" craze, Cronbaugh likened the combination of brew and books as a perfect match. When she noticed a bookstore near the college campus undergoing renovation, she decided to go in and ask about the prospect of adding a coffee shop to the bookstore. The location was, as she learned, ideal.

As the owner of the bookstore would later tell it, "The coffee house became so popular, there was literally no place for anyone to sit. People were sitting on the floor, sipping coffee, and pouring over books."

Connections, Connections, Connections

Sometimes, however, where you are is not as important as who you know. Furniture designer Susan Salzman of Little Folks Art in Santa Monica, California, had those connections, connections, connections. With clients such as Arnold Schwarzenegger and Maria Shriver, Tom Hanks and Rita Wilson, Steven Spielberg and Kate Capshaw, Madonna, Rosie O'Donnell, Dylan McDermott and Shiva Rose, Salzman developed a successful business that she started in her Beverly Hills apartment. Salzman was the assistant to top Hollywood manager Bernie Brillstein when she decided to take a hiatus from script reading and celebrity baby-sitting. She never went back.

Instead, she put the skills she'd learned in a seventh grade shop class to use and began crafting baby furniture for friends. The business moved from her apartment to her parents' garage and, finally in 1991, to a factory where the business resides today. By word of mouth news of her creations spread until Salzman landed her furniture on the movie set of *Father of the Bride 2* with Steve Martin and Diane Keaton.[5] It was no doubt helpful to have Hollywood tongues wagging.

But not all us have the Hollywood connections some of these women have been able to make. I mean, it would be so simple then, wouldn't it? Still, it does not cure all the growing pains of a new business. For example, despite all the celebrities taking their children to Cozy's Cuts for Kids, Wolan still faced an opening day disaster — no water. Krueger-Horn almost went broke before selling her first cookie. Now that her clientele include some of the largest companies in the United States, who could imagine that Krueger-Horn once faced bankruptcy. And in the beginning, Mrs. Fields couldn't give a cookie away to save her life.

Whatever your idea is, have faith in it. Learn from these women. They have all proven that women can do anything in business. Their contributions to our self-esteem, our business communities, our children, and our families have been huge. But the contributions to the future are most valuable. These entrepreneurs offer their advice and share their hard-earned knowledge for one reason — your future success. All of them received help and support from others as they worked to realize their dreams. Each one of them believes we are all in this together and hopes to provide inspiration and encouragement to you.

Chapter 3

Lessons from Mrs. Fields

—

When the idea first came to her, it had seemed so simple. "People love my cookies." Yet, all the surveys and business reports and all the business consultants she spoke with, told Debbi Fields the same thing: America loves crispy cookies, and hers were soft and chewy.

In fact, the whole notion of owning and operating a cookie store was a foreign concept. There were hot pretzel, hot dog, and pizza stores lined along shopping mall walls, but a store that sold exclusively soft, chewy cookies in a crispy cookie-loving society was unfathomable. The only way Fields can explain her determination to forge ahead despite all the skepticism was she knew this cookie was special, and she knew people loved her cookies.

She was used to being different, to being considered the outsider, so this risk-taking attitude was not completely unchartered territory for her. As a child she constantly felt like the outsider in her busy, hectic family. Debbi Sivyer (her maiden name) had her own style in school, from her stand-offish behavior to her own unique dress code.

She was a self-described outsider, so much so, in fact, she requested that she be transferred to a new high school so she could start over. She felt no one would give her a chance at her old school.

She was a poor student, unimpressed with the entire education process, and she had few friends; but she knew she was special. In her book, *One Smart Cookie*, and during our interviews, she said she always felt destined for something. Instead of becoming an introvert as so many kids under those circumstances would have, she became more determined to be herself and find whatever that special something was.

At an early age, Fields discovered the art of marketing herself. As a preteen, she got a job as a ball girl with the Oakland As and to this day remembers how superstar Reggie Jackson treated people. While many of the lesser-known athletes would brush people to the side, she remembers Jackson standing outside the stadium for hours signing autographs for each and every child present. His behavior made a very strong and positive influence on the way she viewed customer service. Because, after all, baseball fans were customers. They bought Reggie Jackson souvenirs, attended the games, and supported his livelihood each time they chanted his name. As Fields points out, Jackson was a savvy businessman who understood this. The others were spoiled prima donnas. "It was basic education. How we should treat each other as human beings."

This philosophy carried over when as a teenager she worked as a sales clerk then as a dolphin trainer at Marine World. Fields was always positive and thrilled to be working with people — and dolphins. But it was in the mid-1970s, when she married her husband, Randy Fields — who ultimately shared her belief in the oversized, chewy cookie — that her life turned around.

Who would have thought that an ex-ball girl and former dolphin trainer could try her hand at business? Yet, Fields used those experiences to come in the back door of business.

To raise capital for their business venture, the Fields put a second mortgage on their house. However, selling the idea to a bank was a whole different story, although not a unique one. Businesswoman after businesswoman describes the agony of seeking financial backing from banks. Fields put it this way, "Banking is nine-tenths instinct. When it comes down to it, bankers have to decide whether you are going to turn them into kings or paupers." How can banks make this kind of decision about people without knowing them?

When the U.S. women's bobsled team tried to secure a loan from several banks, we were selling T-shirts and bumper stickers to turn a profit that would enable us to pay back the loan. What we needed was safe, stable equipment so we wouldn't kill ourselves. We reasoned that if we were going to represent our country in international competition, we ought to have current, semi-functioning equipment. I still remember the phone conversation with a female banker who laughed at the notion of approving a loan to a group of athletes with no business background.

The Fields had a friend at Bank of America who finally agreed to go "against business instincts and make a loan, because they trusted Randy and me to pay back the loan when the business flopped." [1] She was lucky. Now she muses: how could they have possibly turned her away? After all, she had a solid background that fully prepared her to open a cookie store. Having been rescued by dolphins at Marine World before hundreds of people, she was ready to tackle the cookie industry.

There are four things Debbi Fields believes she had going for her at the time.

She was young and naïve

At the tender age of twenty years, she was too young and naïve to fully comprehend all that could have gone wrong. That reason alone is why the experts suggest you make a list of everything that could go wrong, and what you have to lose.

She always believed in herself and her product

As she said over and over again, the cookies were good. People loved her cookies. As part of understanding her market, Fields functioned on pure gut-feeling — a risk that paid off.

She had something special

Over the years, Fields says she has talked to hundreds of business leaders who say the same thing: you must have something special. Was her special something a new kind of cookie, or was it a new kind of store — a cookie store. Was it the combination? To this day, Fields isn't sure, but it was something special that hit the market at the right time.

She was lucky

Because of her husband's reputation, she was able to secure the loan that allowed her to get into the business world. The banker who gave them a break was a part of Randy's network. Both networking and making your own luck are discussed later.

Fields echoed the sentiments of many businesswomen when she said that, once the papers were signed, the loan was secured, and she was ready to begin the very project she had been talking about for so long, there was a long pause.

Now what? What would she call her new business?

On an old episode of "Roseanne," there's a scene in which the family is trying to decide on the perfect name for a new family-owned restaurant. As they rack their brains to find the perfect name, everyone ignores the high-pitched voice of the youngest child, D.J. He insists that he has a name for the business, but is ignored until, at last, he cries out that no one will listen to him. Feeling slightly guilty the family apologizes and smiles patiently at him. "What is it?"

"The Lunch Box," he replies, and everyone is astonished. Ah, the simplicity of a child. It was perfect.

Initially, Mrs. Fields' Cookies was to be called the Chocolate Chippery, then Debbi's Chocolate Chippery, and finally Mrs. Fields' Chocolate Chippery. It was, she explains, just what they were looking for. Elegant, yet friendly with a down home spin. From there, Mrs. Fields' Cookies was born.

Once the name was picked, Fields opened a bank account in that name and began her search for ovens. She searched the classifieds and went to bankruptcy auctions which she describes as terribly confusing. Finally, she turned to a man in a used appliance store to help her locate the perfect ovens for her needs. She spent about $2,000 for equipment.

Opening Day

Opening day arrived. As she retells the story, the anticipation and excitement still in her voice generates smiles.

August 18, 1977, she woke early, did her hair, put on a frilly white apron for the Mrs.-Fields-down-home look, and scuttled off to her new shop. Everything went according to plan. Batches were set out, cooked evenly and thoroughly. They were chewy and perfect. Fields arranged and rearranged all the cookies to her satisfaction. The display was perfect. Presentation, she will assure you, is everything. It was time to open her doors to the cookie eaters of world.

Minutes ticked off the clock. No one came. Fields remained undeterred, smiling at each and every person who walked past the store. An hour passed and she grew worried. The cookies would begin to lose their freshness. One hour turned into two, and Fields decided to take the bull by the horns. She left her post, went around to the front of the store, and offered cookies as samples. Better to have them eaten, sampled for free, than to go to waste, right?

People politely declined, charging past her. Her smile began to fade. What if the studies had been right? What if this wasn't going to work? She wanted to burst into tears. She wanted to crawl into one her freshly customized cabinets. Alas, there was no room for it was filled with all of her newly purchased merchandise, for which she was in debt up to her ears. She called a friend and asked her to come to watch the store in case, she amusingly explains, some poor misguided person should become lost and stumble into her store.

Meantime, Fields became a bona-fide hall-of-fame risk-taker. She took to the streets. Filling a tray with her sam-

Debbi Fields-Rose with a platter of her famous cookies — "presentation is everything"

ple cookies, she went outside the mall onto the busy morning streets and called out, "Free cookies." Initially, she said it was a nightmare. She received the same cold reception as she had inside the mall, but she persisted, walking up to people. Whether they could see that she was about to have a breakdown or suspected there was something special, there were a few brave souls who tried the samples. Guess what? They loved them. As more and more people asked where they could get such a cookie, Fields' faith slowly returned.

Business began to grow, and it was not long before Fields was forced to deal with another unpleasant task: hiring employees. What might seem simple to someone with a degree in business like Cozy Wolan was a difficult task for Fields — so much so that she couldn't bring herself to place an ad in the paper. Instead, she went with her gut feeling again. She struck up a conversation with a store clerk in the mall. She liked the ease with which this woman talked to her customers, and Fields offered her a job. The woman accepted.

In a year's time, Fields was working sixteen-hour days. She hired more employees, and it became clear it was time to expand the store. Expansion meant added expenses, but Fields was not willing to cut personnel costs, and she was certainly not willing to flatten the product by cutting production costs. The only solution was to open a second store which meant signing for another loan.

Growing Pains

In the early years, Mrs. Fields established a standard of excellence that has been the company's hallmark, but there were times when it was difficult to meet her commitment to quality products. In 1978, the California raisin crop was wiped out. There were no raisins to be found at anything but exorbitant prices. All the other restaurants and competitive cookie companies were turning to dates as a substitute.

"I tried a few cookies with dates and really didn't like them," Fields recalls. "I asked, 'Aren't there any raisins anywhere?'" Her vendor told her they were available, but she would pay an almighty price for them. Fields could not bring herself to use dates as a substitute for her cookies, so despite the sky-high prices, she told her vendor to order the raisins. Quality was the most important thing, and her customers appreciated that quality. She continued to produce great cookies, and her clientele continued to buy them.

Her commitment to quality continued, even when a new, half margarine, half butter product came out. It was significantly cheaper. Again, Fields refused to compromise. The best way to make cookies, she says, is with butter. Any substitute changes the flavor and texture of the cookie. She continued to make her cookies with the more expensive, real butter.

One of her first major setbacks came with the notification from the labor department that anyone who was under the age of eighteen years could not operate a washer/mixer. They couldn't even touch it. Suddenly, Fields was faced with some really difficult decisions. It was an immediate notification that demanded immediate action. "What was I suppose to do with the people under eighteen? The mixer is the life of our operation. It is the heart of the kitchen.

The other issue was the fine attached to the notification. A $10,000 fine to be precise. "That was everything to me. Ten thousand dollars was everything to the business. How could I pay it? Then I thought, 'Oh, my Gosh, what am I going to do with all these wonderful people? I can't keep them employed.'"

The bottom line, Fields says, was what it was. She scraped the money together and tried to redirect her team. Still, there was no getting around the fact she would have to let some of the team go. "You must understand that no one was ever hurt [by the mixers], and I really had a hard time with this." As she points out, they were allowed to drive vehicles but considered unqualified to operate mixers.

"I remember talking to the judge. I said, 'This is so unfair.' He said, 'It might be unfair, but it's the law.' I realized right then and there, I had to learn the law. I had to learn everything about this business." In other words, she had to learn the rules of the game.

Fields remains philosophical, reasoning that a difficult situation actually helped her because she had been so naïve about the business world. Because of the fine, Fields was determined to learn everything about the legal aspects of business. "It probably helped me build a better Mrs. Fields." Better yet, she says, it taught her to be proactive rather than reactive.

By age twenty-two, Fields had created this country's first cookie store, successfully operated three stores, and actualized the Baker's Dozen in the cookie world. The Baker's dozen was created to reward the person who, during coffee break, ran down to pick up a dozen cookies for the gang back at the office. Fields included a bonus — a thirteenth cookie in a separate waxed paper wrapper. The idea was the buyer could eat his or her cookie on the way back to the office without disturbing the other cookies that were neatly wrapped in the bag.

What made some people really nervous, however, specifically her investors, was that Fields had not written down any of her recipes on paper. Not a single word. It was all in her head and, as she puts it, "If someone had run a red light, that would have been the end of Mrs. Fields' Cookies."

Until this time, Fields had been making up her own batter mixes in her home and toting them to the shops in plastic ware. However, as the business expanded and she added more stores, not only was this arrangement a bad idea, it was becoming impossible. Ultimately, all the ingredients were prepackaged, which was, Fields says, "The absolute key to expanding a business like Mrs. Fields'." It was yet another stepping stone that taught Fields about planning for the future.

Until this time, there had been no real mission statement. She had only been looking at Mrs. Fields' Cookies, Inc. as a one store project.

Work with Your God Given Talents

While her husband continued to worry about the cost of production, Fields stayed focused on quality. So much so in fact, that they had an operating rule. Randy was not allowed in the kitchen with a calculator. This rule was created when Debbi struck upon a new concept — macadamia nuts with coconuts. The idea came to her while she was lying on the beach in Hawaii staring at a coconut tree. Even though she was supposed to be on a much deserved vacation, her mind never strayed far from her passion. Because macadamia nuts were so expensive, Randy wondered how they could possibly mass produce the scrumptious cookies. But for Mrs. Fields, quality was what mattered most. As with every other cookie she tried, the Coco-Mac cookies were a great success, leading to the development of a vendor relationship in Hawaii for macadamia nuts.

Inadvertently, the exotic nuts inspired another new item in Fields' growing inventory. The nuts were to arrive from Hawaii in halves, but many nuts slipped through, arriving in whole, perfect form. Fields could not stand to see the whole nuts destroyed, so she envisioned a new delicacy. By dipping the nut in cocoa batter, Fields created a new taste sensation that quickly became a big seller at Macy's gourmet candy counter.

Fields stressed over and over, passion is not something that comes from greed. Passion comes from the love of what you are doing. Thank goodness her God-given talent and passion lay in chocolate. Clearly, her love of baking and fine foods and her creativity make up that something special she could never quite put a finger on in her teen-age years.

"People always ask me how to make a million. You can't. Not like that. You have to find something you love." Fields says she is amazed to find that when she asks people what they love, they often don't know. "They don't know what their assets are or what their strengths are. So, the question is, what makes you happy?"

Hard honest work, love of what you do, and love of people is what Fields believes to be the main ingredients for success. And, like making the perfect cookie, you can't delete any of the parts.

"The nuns at Bishop O'Dowd were unanimous in the belief that Debbi Sivyer [before becoming Fields] wasn't much of a math student, but time and tens of thousands of cookies would prove them wrong," Fields half-jokes. It is true that she was not much of a student until she found her passion. The girl who'd struggled through school was suddenly in charge of bookkeeping, inventory, and taxes.

By 1980, Mrs. Fields owned fifteen stores. One decade later, she had over 500 retail stores operating in ten countries throughout the world, and 800 in 2000. This is a remarkable accomplishment because, although women owned approximately forty percent of all businesses in America in 1999, only 1.1 percent of women-owned businesses exported their product or service. The reason, according to the U.S. Department of Commerce's International Trade Administration (ITA), is that women-owned businesses tend to be based on local market interests and demands. Yet, because of Fields' fierce determination and faith in her product and customer service, she was able to expand her oversized, chewy cookie concept overseas.[2]

Fields is the author of three cook books, the host of "Dessert Show" on the TV Food Network, and a speaker for *Fortune* 500 companies seminars.

Much has changed since she opened her first shop, yet her basic philosophy about how to run a business and customer service has stayed the same. It is all about treating people with respect. Fields can name each and every person who has helped her during this twenty-year journey. I noticed that as she spoke to me, she used my name frequently and gave me her full attention, recognizing my importance as a person. Treating people with respect earns respect.

"It's a people business," she says. "Sure, it is a cookie business, but first and foremost, it is always a business about people."

Chapter 4

Cheryl&Co. Makes a Difference

A s a born entrepreneur, Cheryl Krueger-Horn's life story is one of overcoming difficulties, seizing opportunities, and sharing rewards. Perhaps it is because of her mud pie customers and the strong community spirit in her small farming town that Krueger-Horn is a firm believer in sharing her success, giving back to the community in a variety of ways. Mud pies have become gourmet goodies and Krueger-Horn now serves as a model for American business.

Her company, the tremendously successful Cheryl&Co., headquartered in Columbus, Ohio, makes gourmet cookies and desserts, while President and CEO Krueger-Horn makes corporate history. She has gained renown in her community with her innovative business practices and her commitment to public service.

One of the company's most popular projects is "Bring Your Child to Work Day," an expansion of the "Take Your Daughter to Work Day," but with a special twist. Working with the Franklin County [Ohio] Department of Public Services, Cheryl&Co. employees volunteer to have children from county orphanages come to work with them for a day.

The children spend the day with workers, shadowing their new mentors, learning something about a trade skill and having a great time eating cookies. By day's end, the kids learn how to make cookies and how to create a gift box; they make new friends; and, perhaps most important, they hear Krueger-Horn's real life dreams-can-come-true story.

What is the Cheryl Krueger-Horn story? It is about the founder and chief executive officer of one of the highest-grossing and fastest-growing woman-owned businesses in the United States, but it is not a typical how-I-made-my-first-million or how-I-built-a-corporation-in-my-kitchen tale. It's the story of a small-town girl who went to the big city and made good. It's also a story that reminds us we can make our own dream come true. The American dream can come true — with faith, hard work, honesty, and compassion.

Growing up in Bellview, Ohio, Krueger-Horn was fortunate to live in the proverbial village that raises a child — a small town that always pulls together, citizens helping one another during harvest season and sharing each other's good times and bad. The community spirit that surrounded Krueger-Horn as a child became her basic operating philosophy as an adult. That spirit is obvious throughout her company. A majority of Cheryl&Co. employees have a Cheryl story to tell of some connection with Krueger-Horn or her brother, Jim Krueger, who is vice-president of the company.

Krueger-Horn knows all the company's employees and, as she walks through the offices and the plant, she calls them by their first names and asks about their families. She is a working mom and knows first-hand about the frustrations and guilt that come with trying to combine a job and family responsibilities. That is part of the reason that the village model lives at Cheryl&Co. Krueger-Horn expresses her support for company families, saying: "If our employees need to be with their children because they're sick or for a special function, we give them time off. I am adamant about parents going to school functions, even in December when we're running at warp speed here." She acknowledges that the flex time policy earns the company tremendous loyalty and hard work from employees. "It's the right thing to do, and it's good business."

Equity is good business at Cheryl&Co. There are no executive wash rooms here, or separate dining rooms, or even reserved parking. Everybody gets the same treatment, and everybody is expected to give her or his best performance in return.

In 1981, Krueger-Horn and then-business-partner, Caryl Walker, put everything on the line to open their first cookie shop — not yet gourmet — in Columbus, Ohio. With little collateral and no proven product, no bank would give them a loan. Krueger-Horn remembers,

"Their attitude was, 'Why should people buy cookies when they could make them in their home?' They didn't realize that women weren't baking anymore because they were busy with their careers."

Krueger-Horn worked for a major sportswear outlet in New York City and continued to hold that job for security, flying home to Ohio on weekends to work on the start-up of the cookie business. Walker and Jim Krueger managed things during the week. Krueger-Horn still recalls the excitement she felt when they were ready to open their first store.

Everything had been purchased with credit cards or money borrowed from family and friends. Their grand opening was not just the first day of business, it was to be reassurance to all those who had helped that everything was going to work out.

Krueger-Horn, brother Jim Krueger, Director of Operations, and Lisa Henry, Director of Graphics and Promotion, surround Elsie Krueger, whose recipe gave Cheryl&Co. its start — together since 1981

Krueger-Horn, a savvy business woman, had calculated down to the dollar what they should gross by closing time. The shopping mall in which the new store was located had been promoting their grand opening for weeks. Everyone predicted a huge success. It was a Thursday night and Krueger-Horn had paced nervously all day at work. Finally, at 11:00 P.M., Krueger-Horn called Walker from New York and got some unexpected and unwanted news. "So, how did it go?" Krueger-Horn asked, nearly breathless in anticipation.

"It didn't," responded a defeated sounding Walker. Batch after batch of the cookies didn't rise. Every cookie was flat as a pancake. Walker never even opened the doors.

Krueger-Horn flew home. All weekend the two entrepreneurs went over Krueger-Horn's grandmother's recipes to no avail. The mall owners were furious. Now, Krueger-Horn and Walker were operating on borrowed time as well as borrowed money. For weeks, they measured, re-measured, baked, and prayed. The outcome was always the same.

Then Krueger-Horn went to seek advice from a chef she knew about at the old Hilton East Hotel in Columbus. "Look, you don't know me," she began her plea. In the end, the chef agreed to go to her store and try to figure out what was going wrong. He quickly discovered that it was a faulty scale. The scale they were using to transform Krueger-Horn's grandmother's basic recipe for a few dozen cookies into 50- to 100-pound quantities did not calculate correctly. It was easily fixed but caused a very scary beginning for Cheryl&Co. "We were almost finished before we ever opened our doors," Krueger-Horn now muses.

But open the doors they did, plus six more stores during the next three years. Cheryl&Co. was steadily on the rise. Then, in 1985, another set-back occurred, one that was far more devastating than the flat cookies. Walker was diagnosed with cancer. Described as a real health nut, a top finisher in the Columbus marathon for four consecutive years, Walker refused chemotherapy or other medical treatment, turning instead to health crystals. Krueger-Horn insisted that Walker move in with her. From that point on, Krueger-Horn and her brother Jim took care of Walker until her death in May 1986.

Walker's death was devastating to the Kruegers and to the new company, but it was also a turning point in Krueger-Horn's life and for Cheryl&Co. She quit her job in New York and put all her energies into developing the business. Her innovative ideas and ingenuity turned a propitious small business into a smashing success.

Like Pudge Kleinkauf, Krueger-Horn was forced to redirect her life. For both women, directly and indirectly, cancer was the impetus for leaving the security of their current lives and becoming risk-takers. Both women, suddenly aware of how precious life can be, were ready to play the game — and win.

Up to this point, Cheryl&Co. had been a hard sell. Most malls already had a Mrs. Fields' Cookies. Krueger-Horn was a small competitor without a unique product or a necessary service, but she was not about to be stopped now. She contacted Ohio State University professor and marketing expert Roger Blackwell and "traded some cookies for advice." The advice resulted in new marketing techniques and a catalogue to sell gourmet desserts. That was when the orders began to roll in. There were no gourmet cookie and cake stores in shopping malls and no gourmet foods presented in such an attractive and fashionable manners in mail order catalogues — a reflection, no doubt, of Krueger-Horn's fashion house background. Cheryl&Co. had found its niche.

In the intervening ten years, sometimes frenzied and always exhilarating, Cheryl&Co has grown by leaps and bounds: $10 million net sales in 1994; $18 million in 1996; over $24 million in 1999, and projected sales of $34 million for 2000. Regular customers include: US Airways, Delta Air Lines; American Air Lines; Cookers Restaurants; General Electric; Ruby Tuesday's restaurants; Bob Evan's restaurants; Williams Sanoma, Bank One; The Limited; Kodak; The Gap; numerous hospitals, cafeterias, and schools; and other companies that sell cookies, pies, and cheesecakes through their gourmet catalogues. One of those companies is Gourmet Gifts, a Columbus-based business.

Enter Valerie Coolidge. As the creator and owner of Gourmet Gifts, Coolidge began her career selling delicious rum and amaretto cakes for the holidays. But, like other businesswomen, Coolidge began to have growing pains. "I had some really big accounts, but I almost lost my largest cake customer in the first year because they didn't want to give people a liquor cake. They didn't think it was politically correct, so I told them, 'I have a really great non-alcoholic orange cake.' That saved the sale." Still, her liquor cakes were big sellers.

As Coolidge moved into her second successful season, she received some more unpleasant news: "I found out it was illegal [in Ohio] to make liquor cakes." In fact, it is illegal in all but eleven states. "I was very discouraged by that. And no lawyer would touch it with a ten-foot pole. The fact that I live in a dry county didn't help matters, either," she laughs.

Although the non-alcoholic orange cake was a big seller, orders for her liquor cakes kept coming in. Coolidge was forced to research new recipes if she was to stay competitive. Like Krueger-Horn, Coolidge understood that she needed a niche, something that would set her apart from the bakery down the street.

That was when she discovered the chocolate covered spoon. "I didn't invent it," she says. "I only improved it. There was a company in Texas who made them, but the quality was pretty poor. They did mass quantities and didn't use pure chocolate. I wanted to make a pure gourmet chocolate spoon with the swirl look and put them in hand made baskets. They have more class which appeals to the gourmet and gift shops."

It was a look that would eventually catch the sharp eye of Krueger-Horn, but at first Coolidge had a difficult time getting to the CEO. This is another example of what Cozy Wolan says, "Usually the people saying *no* are simply the people who don't have the authority to say *yes*."

Instead, Coolidge turned to the Columbus Gift Shop — an open market for business hopefuls. "But the problem was they encouraged you to sell fifteen percent under the market value. But my product was very time consuming. I individually created each spoon. I just couldn't take that kind of ticket slashing."

It was not until Coolidge got involved with the Women's Network of Entrepreneurial Training (WNET) through the Greater Columbus Chamber of Commerce's Small Business Development Center that Coolidge finally met her mentor. Krueger-Horn immediately placed a large order for Coolidge's chocolate covered spoons for her gourmet shops and gift catalogues. The relationship between Cheryl&Co. and Gourmet Gifts was cemented.

Being a mentor is just one of the responsibilities Krueger-Horn feels as a business leader and member of her community. Rather than talk about herself, she talks about the hows of her business: how she got her ideas, how she got backing, and how she overcame obstacles. Instead of singing her own praises, she talks about what went wrong. The successes, she believes, are self-evident. Instead, it was the costly mistakes, the personal disasters, the unanticipated calamities that made Cheryl&Co. what it is today. It is about how Cheryl&Co. turned disasters into learning processes that created today's multi-million dollar corporation.

The disasters were plentiful. As Cheryl learned even with a feasibility study — discussed in the next chapter — there are unforeseen risks. The purpose of the feasibility study is to minimize risks, and it is critical to success. However, even a businesswoman as astute and organized as Krueger-Horn could not foresee all the disasters, both personal and business, that were to come.

Sometimes in business, no matter how much preparation is put into the start-up, misfortune sweeps in like a tornado leaving nothing but debris in its wake. There were times when cash flow problems prompted Krueger-Horn to put the payroll on her credit card. There was the trusted employee who stole more than $130,000 to remodel his own home. When he skipped town, Krueger-Horn and her small staff learned a lot about the law and the judicial system. Then there was the unpredictable loss of $250,000 when a store in New York failed because of the shopping mall's ties to ex-Philippine president Ferdinand Marcos. Also, there were failed marriages.

Krueger-Horn says her marriages were immediately under stress because of the company and its importance in her life. She feels that the connection between a women's professional success and her personal relationships is complex. The basic issue, she says, is that most men are still not prepared to handle women's successes in the business world, especially the women in their lives.

Krueger-Horn describes how she and John Green, former husband and father of her son, had to learn to share parenthood, from agreeing who was going to wash the baby's hair and who was going to trim his nails and who was getting up in the middle of the night, to setting the drop-off and pick-up schedule for school. Green, whom Krueger-Horn met at Cheryl&Co., is still with Cheryl's Cookies. He played a major role in establishing the tremendously successful corporate and wholesale divisions of the company, including landing some major accounts, such as several airlines.

Lessons Learned

Krueger-Horn learned that her personal relationships would suffer from time to time because of her commitment to her company, but she was willing to make that sacrifice. As soon as she put her plan on paper, she jumped into action. She was proactive. She understood that the company would have to come first if it was going to make it. She dedicated herself 100 percent to making her dream a reality. She also learned some professional relationships would be strained. She could not afford to be passive as a businesswoman.

"I know I'm difficult when it comes to business negotiating. I will negotiate what's best for the business, period. I'm also very, very tough on employees in the organization. If you don't perform, you're fired — it's as simple as that.

"Just getting by is not what we're about. You have to perform at the highest level to have a job here. When you do, you are paid incredibly well. If you don't, you aren't paid at all. Some people think that's insensitive, but I'm the one signing on the bottom line, and I wouldn't ask anybody to do anything I wouldn't do myself." Or haven't done already.

Even her greatest admirers will admit under some pressure that Krueger-Horn is sometimes intense and can be hard to keep up with. But then, ask the Boy Scouts of America about the Krueger-Horn *tough* image, or members of the Columbus churches, or the local police officer who needed a liver transplant — all have benefited from her support. Or ask Columbus school children about Krueger-Horn's "Cookies for *As*" program, perhaps the ultimate in a business-education alliance. Any child who earns an *A* may bring her or his report card to any Cheryl's Cookies store and receive a free cookie.

It is no wonder this role model is named in *Who's Who Among Outstanding Americans* and her company has received multiple awards for integrity in business. In 1999, she was named *Working Woman*'s Entrepreneur of the Year.

The Cheryl&Co. mission statement is simply, "To be the best gourmet food and gift company ever." Krueger-Horn sums up her approach to life and business in one telling statement, "Our success is attributed to three critical ingredients on which you cannot place a price tag: our customers, our associates, and our reputation."

Her early experiences on her family's farm, working with a close-knit community, laid the groundwork for the kind of company Krueger-Horn envisioned Cheryl&Co. to be. Linking baked foods with childhood memories and considering the time-intensive environment of a busy home, especially at holiday time, this cookie set gives parents and children an opportunity to make cookies together. It's all there — cookie dough, cookie cutters, red and green sprinkles, baking instruction, and the famous Cheryl&Co. buttercream icing. "Times change," Krueger-Horn says, "but we can preserve some of those parts of our heritage by developing new ways to pass on traditions." Tradition, loyalty, and social consciousness are what Cheryl&Co. and Cheryl Krueger-Horn are all about.

Can a cookie really make a difference in your community? Having met Cheryl Krueger-Horn and Debbi Fields personally, I can tell you the answer is a resounding, yes!

Chapter 5

What Level of Risk
Are You Ready to Take?

B eing a risk-taker is what entrepreneurialism is all about, right? But, what if you were to learn that some of the most successful business people were the least likely people to take risks?

In interviews with professional women and entrepreneurs, books on women in business and management, studies regarding the behavioral differences of women in business and the support (or lack thereof) they receive, the expression *risk-taker* must have come up several hundred times. There is a distinct correlation in our minds between success and taking risks. Also, this advice was given over and over again in various forms:

> If you have an idea that makes you feel good, research it, write out a mission statement, talk to the experts, find the right location, be wary of naysayers, and trust your own instinct.

Yet, even when following this advice, many women fail to realize their dreams. Several women talked about being laughed out of banks, being unable to find financial backing, investors, or sponsors, and how sparse federal grants are for women in business, despite all the promises.

Why? I asked. What's missing? Are we doing something wrong?

"The approach is all wrong," says Ed Moldt, director of the John Papa-John Entrepreneurial Center at the University of Iowa. Moldt breaks away from the standard advice. "The question," he says, "should not be,

'Are you a risk-taker?' It's the wrong question. We should be asking, 'What level of risk are you willing to take? What kind of risk do you think you can take and be comfortable with?' The ranges may be from a bungee jumper to someone who says, 'Hey, I can't take those kind of risks, I have a family and obligations.'"

Therefore, Moldt says, it is a matter of finding the business that fits your risk profile. While lots is said and written about risk-taking, that is not the only — or even the most important — quality for a successful business person. Debbi Fields agrees. It is not for the money or the thrill of taking risks that you try to build a business. There must be something inherent within that you want or need to share — an idea that can make life easier or more enjoyable for yourself and others. Starting a business is not, Moldt says, simply for the thrill of taking risks. "If you told me you were going to

Ed Moldt ~ John PapaJohn Entrepreneurial Center, University of Iowa

mortgage your house, I would ask why you are willing to do that? The risk is too great. I would ask you if you've looked for alternatives."

Have You Done a Feasibility Study?

Experts like Moldt distinguish between being a risk-taker and being reckless. You can take risks in a responsible way by having all the facts you need to decide about the business. That's where a feasibility report comes in. Just what is a feasibility study, you ask?

I asked the very same question. It's funny that I would have to ask. After all, I have talked to dozens and dozens of the most successful business women in this country; poured over books, studies, and reports;

talked to experts on Wall Street and representatives of women's business organizations and nary a one mentioned a feasibility study. I went back to ask and discovered some of the women with whom I spoke were completely unaware of such studies and many others were aware of the study but had not done one.

Tara Cronbaugh did, however. In fact, it was because of Cronbaugh that I discovered Moldt. Cronbaugh wondered, "What is a business proposal, and how do I write one?" Cronbaugh searched for some help and found Moldt's sixteen-week course for entrepreneurs that would answer all her questions.

After I talked to Cronbaugh, I called Moldt myself, wanting to learn about those valuable sixteen weeks. Once again, I found a remarkable supporter. Like the aspiring businesspeople in his classes, Moldt has good ideas that he is willing to share. In fact, Moldt's business is spreading success. Here is some of his invaluable advice.

What Is A Feasibility Study

How do you mitigate risks? You can't get rid of all the risks, but you can minimize them. "That is the heart of entrepreneurialism," Moldt says. And that is what a feasibility study is all about. It is intended to answer the questions: this thing I want to do, is it do-able and at what financial and personal cost?

"The idea that you have to take a lot of risks is stupid," says Moldt. "Those of us who have been doing this our whole lives know this does not have to be. That is what bankers, insurance companies, vendors, suppliers, and brokers are for. In talking with them, you can eliminate as much of the risk factor as possible, so if you're wrong, you can always back out."

The thrust of Moldt's entrepreneurial course is to introduce his students to the concept of how a business is created. The students are asked to identify a business they are interested in then to figure out how they would finance it.

That was exactly what Cronbaugh needed to know. She knew she wanted to own and run a coffee shop. Once she made that decision, she had to prepare a feasibility report to see if her business would pay for itself. It is here, Moldt says, the majority of his students usually find their ideas are not so good after all. "Once they do a feasibility study, most find it is best to move on to a new idea. We want them to get very good at making these studies and to be comfortable with [letting go of] the ones that don't meet their standards." Too often, he says, people stay with an idea no matter what. They feel compelled to stay loyal to their original idea, a kind of a captain-going-down-with-the-sinking-ship mentality. Instead, Moldt wants his students to be able to think fast on their feet and restructure or abandon ideas that don't work. "Some are lucky and pass on the first hit. They know what the capital is going to be; they can see the returns and know the risks."

For those who do find their businesses, be it on the first or tenth try, they are then asked to make a presentation to the class. Remember the naysayers? This is where Moldt says they are vital to the business process. The class is expected to ask questions of and suggest potential problems to the presenter. It is all too easy for eager new businesspeople to overlook even the most obvious of problems.

"The class acts as consultants. They ask them [the presenters] questions like, What could you do to change this or that? What could you

Tara Cronbaugh behind the counter of the Iowa City Coffee Company.

do to make this better? We try to give them red flags that will pop up from time to time." Over the course of the sixteen weeks, the students are able to see several dozen different feasibility studies and make the ultimate decision: do I want to be in my own business? As Moldt points out, often students see just how much work is involved and opt to work for someone else.

In Cronbaugh's case, however, she hit the nail right on the head. While she appreciates Moldt's view of the world of entrepreneurship from the logical side, she believes there is something to Fields' claims of owning a gut-feeling. Even Moldt agrees that Cronbaugh could not be swayed. She knew she wanted to own and run a coffee shop. She knew that despite whatever she turned up in her feasibility study, she would go through with her dream. Still, the study allowed her to better prepare herself for what was to come.

Conduct a Feasibility Study

As Moldt explains, only by answering some very important questions can you determine whether your idea is as good as you think and will suit your lifestyle. Perhaps if Valerie Coolidge had performed a feasibility report, she might have truly understood how much work and time was going to go into the gourmet foods business. Admittedly, Coolidge says the start-up of Gourmet Gifts was fun and exciting, but the everyday deadlines became a strain on her family as the business expanded, which is why she sold it. Be brutally honest as you answer the next six questions, taking into account your family, friends, financial situation, degree of dedication, determination, and passion.

1. Identify Your Chosen Field

If you could choose anything in the world to do, what would it be? When you think you know exactly what you want to do, learning what is involved in starting your own business becomes important. Moldt says that for every person who says she or he would like to be in business for themselves, there are that many more who discover they do not want the kind of responsibility, hard work, and long hours that go along with being one's own boss.

If owning your business is still what you want, however, you must ask yourself what it is you are really good at. As Diane Jacobs of

When maestro Diane Jacobs applies her skills, the music is good enough to eat

The Cakeworks says, "You can succeed when you follow a God-given talent." For her, making and designing cakes was something she did as a pre-teen. Jacobs is a firm believer in divine guidance and says we all have a calling for something. Something. But what? It must be something that holds your passion, something you know you can spend twenty hours a day doing and never tire of it.

2. Define Your Boundaries

You must answer, for yourself, all of these questions:

- What is it I want to do?
- Where and how do I want to live?
- What do I need?
- How can I get what I need?
- How long will it take me?

So many of us define ourselves by where we are today, where we are physically situated. At the time I interviewed Moldt, he was busily writing a proposal to the University of Iowa, suggesting that other departments within the university encourage students to take his entrepreneurial classes.

To be able to introduce the concept of business to engineering or chemistry majors or to students in the performing arts could open new doors of opportunity for all of them. As Moldt puts it, "How many college graduates enter the real world only to discover they want nothing to do with their majors. The show of hands would be staggering. But what if music majors learned how to open their own music stores or chemistry majors could use their knowledge from college to identify a market that has a need, create a new product, and apply their degree toward building their own business. Suddenly, these people are saying, 'Oh, I guess I don't have the boundaries I thought I had.'"

Who would have thought an ex-dog trainer and bobsledder would have entered the world of business? Who would have thought an ex-ball girl and dolphin trainer would be giving speeches around the country to *Fortune* 500 companies? Only by looking outside our boxes and analyzing our résumés are we able to recognize how to apply our different talents toward creating our own futures.

For women like Cronbaugh, there were simply no boundaries at all. She was a pit bull latching on to an idea and refusing to let it go. For her, the next step was how to build the structure of a business around the idea.

3. Build a Business Around Your Fantasy

You must ask yourself: is there a need or a niche? In the cases of Mrs. Fields' Cookies and Cronbaugh's coffee house, others did exist. Fields realized, however, that there were no soft, oversized, chewy cookies on the market. That was her niche. Cronbaugh saw there were absolutely no coffee houses like the one she fell in love with in California on or near the University of Iowa's campus. There was certainly an opportunity in both instances.

For Jenny Craig Weight Loss Centers, the Miracle Mop, and F&B Transportation (for children of working parents), there was a definite need. For Annie's Edibles, The Cakeworks, and Illume Candles, there was a demand. People always want tasty dinners, desserts, and candlelight. It was a matter of how to market the ideas to make them work, to be competitive.

It all comes down to a simple question: how can I package this opportunity in a way that I can enjoy what I am doing and make a success of it? A simple question with a complex answer.

4. Create Your Own Feasibility Study

Moldt calls this the visionary stage. Rather than calling entrepreneurs risk-takers, Moldt believes defining yourself as a visionary is much more credible and will generate more confidence in what you are doing.

As he emphasizes in his classes, this stage has nothing to do with making money. To suggest otherwise is unrealistic. At this stage, you cannot guess at what the expenses and revenues will be. It is here that business hopefuls tend to make their biggest mistakes, often overlooking some important steps. This is the point in your thinking you must consider exactly what you want to do and where you want to do it — the important location issue.

You must ask yourself:

- What will separate my business from others that are similar?
- What will make me unique?

It is time to talk to other business owners and managers. This is when you might begin to redefine your original idea. Also, you need to talk to potential customers.

- Do other people think I have a good idea?
- Does anyone actually want my product or service?

5. Develop Your Business Plan

Now that you've determined there is a need or demand for your product or idea, developed the idea into a vision, and begun the research to determine if it is, in fact, feasible for your lifestyle and needs, it is time to move the idea from a vision to reality. That means the cold, hard numbers. You must determine exactly what the costs will be to get your business up and running and the least amount of money needed to keep it running.

Ask about costs of equipment rentals, building-space leases, personnel costs, and retail overhead. In Cronbaugh's classes she was asked, "Can you afford this business?" and "How much is needed each day, week, and month to keep your doors open for business?" Cronbaugh did detailed research for her feasibility study, but made avoidable mistakes when she chose to skip some important steps. For instance, had she done more research on how to manage a business, she would have found it easier to deal more effectively with her employees.

Because many people focus on what they can or want to make as a profit, Moldt says, "They overlook the possibilities for everyday calamities." In Wolan's case, the day she opened her Cozy's Cuts for Kids hair salon, there was no water. Krueger-Horn had flat cookies. There were immediate, unanticipated losses.

By collecting data from other businesses, suppliers of equipment, leasing companies, vendors, and store managers, Cronbaugh was able to assess what her monthly costs would be and further break them down so she could understand what she needed to sell each day to keep her doors open.

Determining a proper location was vital to how much business she would be able to generate. By setting up shop in a bookstore — an already established and well-respected fixture on campus — she virtually guaranteed herself a set number of customers per day.

6. Know the Real Myth about Being a Risk-Taker

To be a risk-taker means to take a deep breath, give a final nod of the head, and plunge in, knowing your idea is so solid it is worth all risks. You sign on the dotted line, committing yourself to a second mortgage, a bank loan, or some other kind of legal commitment to pay a price all-too-dear should you go belly up. However, that's what makes the pulse rate soar and adds an extra thrill to the game of entrepreneurship. In the bobsled world we call it the thrill of the spill. There's always a fifty percent chance you're going to land on your head and break some bones.

Instead, Moldt cautions, we should rethink this strategy. Behaving as a visionary is a better strategy. Always look to the future, yet know where the back door is. "Have some flexibility. Always leave yourself as many outs as possible. That is the true entrepreneur. What happens if you are wrong? If you are wrong and it has cost you everything you own, you can only play the game once."

Like Fields, Moldt views this aspect of business as a sport. There is the thrill of competition and the exhilaration of finding success, but it is important to understand all the rules and consequences. Know how to crash. Fields learned many of her rules as she played the game. Fortunately, her perseverance (and luck) paid off. Yet, for all the books filled with success stories, there are ten times as many stories of people kept from fulfilling their dreams by poor luck, oversight, or misunderstandings.

"There are a lot of people out there who believe that in order to start a company, you have to invest hundreds of thousands of dollars. Frankly, I don't think that's necessary," says Terry Neece. She ought to know. Like Moldt, Neece believes that leaving yourself a way out is the best way to go into a business. When she was just

Neece to speak to Senate about small business issues. *(L to R)* Senator Newt Gingrich, Congressman Jim Talent (R. MO); Terry Neese; Phyllis Hill-Slater, NAWBO past president; Whitney Johns-Martin, NAWBO President.

twenty-two years old, broke, and divorced with a small child, Neece struck a deal that allowed her that back door. She went to the vendors of a company she previously ran — it folded when its business license expired — and convinced them to give her thirty days to pay them back. Then she made the same deal for office furniture with a company in bankruptcy. She was certain she could turn a profit in that short amount of time.

She rented some office space, moved in her on-credit furniture and supplies, and created her own personnel service. Thirty days later, she kept her end of the bargain, and eighteen months later, she turned enough profit to buy her own building. Had it not worked, she would have had a much lower risk than usual because, as Neece points out, "I didn't want to have to borrow money." That foresight and initiative in convincing her vendors to give her short-term support reduced her initial expenses and helped her succeed.

How to Make Your Own Luck

Comedian Bill Cosby does an amusing skit about his daughter who must have figured she'd done her part by attending the classes he paid for because she sat on his couch, watched television, and ate for two months after graduating. He couldn't figure out why since she could be anything she wanted to be. Then, he says, he learned her plan was for prospective businesses to come knock on her door and beg her to work for them. The degree she held meant nothing with this strategy; it could have been a Ph.D. or a G.E.D.

Creating your own luck or destiny requires action. A degree is little more than an unfinished mission statement, and for most entrepreneurs, a temporary one at that. It's a good start, but degree or no degree, you must use what you know to learn what you don't know. Banks are not going to come to you begging for business.

You Don't Need a Background in Business

Debbi Fields felt that she was in over her head. She was just making cookies. Even now she remembers the feeling she had when she tried to sell her idea to banks and investors. The smiles, she recalls, were so patronizing. Wolan, Krueger-Horn, and Jenai Lane all had the same feeling. Somehow what they were doing was less than important. One banker asked Krueger-Horn, "Why would anyone buy your cookies when they could make them at home?" And when Mangano tried to sell the Miracle Mop, doors closed all around her. "They said it was just another mop. Men didn't get it. They don't mop."

But the successes of these women validate a comment Moldt made to me. "Give me the lowest technology there is, and I'll be in business a lot longer than most." For Krueger-Horn, readjusting the scale for her baking soda took less than twenty minutes. Rounding up stray tumbleweeds involved good running shoes and sturdy boxes for Linda Katz.

It is the most simple ideas, those that make our lives less complicated, that make us smile or feel good about ourselves. It is simple ideas that are allowing these women to grin all the way to the bank. They did not have to be business tycoons or have their Ph.D.s in chemistry or engineering to build multi-million dollar empires. As Mangano reminds us, "You don't have to be an engineer to design something. Just put it [the idea] on paper."

"Some of the most unimaginative people I've known are business majors," Moldt laughs. Imagine if we could capture the creativity and imagination of liberal arts students, teach them about creating feasibility studies, and watch them go as they discover what their passions are and how they could make a dream become a reality. But, until now, entrepreneurialism has been strictly categorized as Business. Yuck. The dreaded *B* word.

Analyze the Feasibility of Your Idea

The primary purpose of a feasibility study is to flush out as many risks as possible, so you will be able to attain a high level of confidence for yourself and your lenders. You want to prove to them you can pay them back. In addition, you want to know you can really do it.

Until you can produce a low-risk report, you need to continue to reanalyze or to find an entire new approach to your business idea. Don't just mindlessly keep marching forward. How do you know if something is unrealistic or not feasible if you don't talk to other business leaders?

It is important for you, just as Moldt's students do in the classroom environment, to talk with people who will ask you how you can make things better or make yourself different from the competition. It is important to get different perspectives on your business.

"Take your proposal to other businesses," Moldt suggests. "It does not have to be in the area [in which] you are [interested]. A business is a business is a business. You want to ask them, 'How do I have the fewest risks and the highest return?' Find successful people in your community and ask them to look at your study.

But be prepared to hear that it won't work or that something requires modification." It is all too common for business hopefuls to ignore naysayers, writing them off simply as negative individuals. But there is a difference between your Uncle Bob who mutters nothing ever works and a successful business person who has spotted a hole in your business theory. "The failure rate [of business] usually comes about when the person does not want to hear that something won't work. They find that their dream will not come true, and they choose to ignore the advice."

Moldt believes talking to business leaders is an important part of the process of doing a feasibility study. "They will tell you the truth whether you want to hear it or not. It's not personal for them. Just business. It is relatively easy to find people in your community who have succeeded and failed in business ventures. You should talk to both."

As for Cronbaugh, Moldt says the faculty at the University of Iowa's entrepreneur program tried to get her to slow down. "We tried to get her to wait until she was able to get more experience. She was going in with more things to be learned and, as a result, she had some problems." Cronbaugh knew what she wanted to do and, once the ball got rolling, it was hard for her to slow it down. However, because of the network she'd built with her professors, she would not be abandoned. "It took us a long time to iron out some of the problems. She was up to her armpits in alligators. You can't imagine how much coffee we drank," Moldt muses. "But she was fast on her feet and was willing to change the way she did things. She is someone who continues to learn. She was able to figure out what worked and what didn't and modify her behavior."

These things, Moldt says, are the key to whether you will survive your first days as an entrepreneur. The term risk-taker doesn't apply to Tara Cronbaugh. Through her own hard work, feasibility plan, perseverance, and flexibility — and a little help from her friends — she made it work. She is a visionary.

You will find in the Resources section dozens of organizations prepared to help you make your next move: talking to banks and investors.

Use these and all other resources available to you. Especially important, talk to as many people as you can.

When You Must Go to a Bank

As you have read, many women have gone to their families to borrow money rather than face the heavy restrictions of a bank or the humiliation of being laughed out of an investor's door. No matter how well they do, most new businesses can't possibly make the kind of return that a venture capitalist expects, so Moldt believes it is unrealistic to put much time or energy into that pursuit.

However, a new business hopeful can obtain grants or borrow money from institutions, private organizations, or banks, as Lane and Cronbaugh did. They worked within the structure to obtain loans from organizations willing to help out new businesses. The resources at the back of this book can get you started in the right direction. Also, *The Rule Book of Business Plans for Startups* by Roger C. Rule is an excellent guide, offering step-by-step instructions for researching and preparing your start-up business presentation.

In addition, Moldt explains, there are angel networks (individuals who want to invest in new companies in which they can become involved) within most major universities, and there are organizations ready and willing to help entrepreneurs. Unlike venture capitalists who tend to invest a great deal of money with little or no involvement, angel network investors are often only three or four people who come together and pool anywhere from $20,000 to $50,000 for investments close to home — where they can kick the tires, so to speak. They want something very personal. Angel network investors can be ideal for someone with a start-up company because they can lower your risk factors and provide you with partners who are personally interested in your success. The downside can be their personal involvement and influence in your, now shared, venture.

Even as venture capitalists shower billions of dollars on startup businesses, only a very small portion of those monies is being invested in the estimated 9.1 million businesses owned by women. The numbers say it all. Women own thirty-eight percent of all businesses, yet they only receive two percent of the money invested by venture capital firms, according to the NFWBO and Wells Fargo & Co. For this reason, a new true-to-it's name angel network emerged. Count-Me-In.org was launched May 11, 2000 with the sole purpose of giving more opportunities and power to women entrepreneurs.[1]

"Access to credit and capital continues to be an issue to women, particularly to women of color and those in small businesses," says co-creator Nell Merlino. Merlino and partners were documenting the disturbingly low statistics involving women entrepreneurs as recipients of venture capital. Finally, she decided it was time to do something about this disparaging situation.

"Why not solve the problem," she asked herself. While Merlino concedes Count-Me-In.org. may not solve the problem entirely, they are well on their way to evening the playing field. With sponsors like American Express (the first to come on board), Verizon Wireless, Crown Hotels . . . and many "friendly family foundations," Count-Me-In.org. has been able to reach out a hand to many women. By September 2000, the organization approved fifty loans.

Kristy Eaton was the first lucky applicant to qualify for $3,500 to begin her own cake baking business, A Matter of Taste. Already featured on the Today Show, Eaton is off to a great start. She had been surfing the web looking for lucky lotto numbers when she stumbled onto the *Count-Me-In.org* website. The rest, as they say, is history. "Our on going goal," Merlino says, "is to put as many women in business as possible. We want to demonstrate to banks that women are very viable business owners who are great people to lend money to."

Both Lane of Respect, Inc. and Coolidge of Gourmet Gifts found their sponsors and mentors through local women's entrepreneurial chapters. Whatever organization you approach, you must have your feasibility study and business proposal — or business plan — ready and available, so they can see what you have done to minimize risks.

However, as Vanessa Freytag, banking executive for Bank One in Cincinnati, Ohio, reminds us, there is always risk. "Even in conducting this feasibility report," she says, "there is a risk. Certainly, you can minimize the risks. In fact, this is exactly what the banks want to see. But if there were no risks involved, why would banks evaluate credit history?" Because seven out of every ten new businesses fail, banks want to see a business plan with all aspects of your feasibility report referenced in the appropriate sections of your plan.

When to Protect Your Concept

As mentioned before, if you have an actual product prototype, be sure to get a nondisclosure form signed before you make your presentation. Too many inventors have lost an idea (and millions of dollars) because they were too trusting of those to whom they showed their prototype. Cronbaugh did not have to worry about someone running wild in the streets of Iowa City with the idea of a coffee shop. But, Lane lost an entire collection of necklaces she designed to a well-established company in Hollywood because it never occurred to her that such a prestigious company would rip off her designs. It was a hard lesson learned.

Remember that an idea is not property. You cannot patent an idea, although there are means for protecting your ideas. One way is to require that a nondisclosure statement be signed by the other party before you reveal your idea.

A lawyer can draw up a nondisclosure statement, or examples can be found in your local library. Briefly, the documents state:

- You are the originator of the disclosed idea or invention.
- The other party has not thought of the idea.
- She or he will not use the idea without your permission.
- She or he will not reveal your idea to anyone else.
- She or he will regard your idea as highly confidential.

You must also write to the Commissioner of Patents, Washington, D.C. 20231, stating:

1. You are the originator of the idea or invention you describe, and
2. You request that the attached description of the idea be accepted under the Disclosure Document Program and preserved for a period of two years.

The Patent Office will assign a Disclosure Document number. For more information on protecting and developing your ideas, consult the *Develop and Market Your Creative Ideas*, Second Edition, by Dale A. Davis. A third edition will be coming out in the fall of 2001.

Leasing Considered Creditworthy by Investors

By leasing her equipment and renting rather than buying space in a building, Cronbaugh was able to show in her business plan she could absolve all business costs quickly if she needed to. She could simply terminate the leasing contract and have the company pick up their equipment to end that relationship. A lease with a landlord is broken easily enough; but if you own property, finding the back door is not as easy. "If the location is bad or the company is going under, you are stuck with the long-term contractual agreements," warns Moldt. "That can be very damaging."

Moldt contends that no one should ever buy a computer. "No sooner do you take it out of the box than there is another one on the market faster and more efficient. You want to be a virtual company, owning as little as possible. As the expression goes, 'Keep your cap on and your knees bent.' You need to be able to change as quickly as the market, and the market is always changing."

Twelve Reasons to Start Your Own Business

Before you invest one dime of your own good money, there are some factors you must establish. We have all taken those fun self-help quizzes in magazines that promise to teach us about our personalities. They are entertaining and basically utter nonsense. However, it is important to be brutally honest with yourself when you consider the items on these two lists of twelve reasons — to start or not to start your own business.

As banking executive Vanessa Freytag warns, most potential entrepreneurs are so excited about their new business idea, few think through all the scenarios of failure or disappointment. Ponder the following reasons why and why not to begin a new business venture, adapted from an article by Bob Weinstein.[2] If you grade yourself accurately, you could save your business, your wallet, and much more.

1. Finding Your Passion

Starting your own business can be extremely difficult and stressful; however, if it is something you love to do, you will have fun with the challenge. For women like Cronbaugh and Fields, every obstacle was greeted with enthusiasm. As Confucius once said, "If you love what you do, you'll never work a day in your life."

2. Finding Your Niche

Whether you have discovered a completely new product or service or have simply found a way of making something better, you need to ask yourself what makes your idea special. Will it be wanted or needed by the market you will focus on?

3. Identifying the Pay-Off

The purpose of a feasibility report is to limit the risk. Can you make a living at this? Wolan and Krueger-Horn continued to work at their jobs while they worked out their business plans. Cronbaugh invested in a class for entrepreneurs to learn how to create a business proposal before leaping in. Ask yourself, will your idea turn a profit? Then outline how it will.

4. Activating Your Determination and Independence

How many budding entrepreneurs have had doors shut in their faces as they began their adventure into the business world? Still, each time Wolan was told "no," she found someone else to say "yes." You must have drive, determination, and diligence to succeed as an entrepreneur.

5. Learning from Your Mistakes

Reed refuses to see her mistakes as anything but temporary setbacks. In most cases, mistakes proved to be tremendous learning tools. As Fields reminds us, for each obstacle she faced, she became more determined to learn the rules of the game.

6. Making Your Dream Come True

Many successful entrepreneurs fantasized about running the businesses they now lead. Fields speculates it is something inherent in you. If the passion is truly there, you will make it happen. Kristin Penta was dreaming of making her own lipsticks and making rose-petal water when she was just a little girl. Now she is highly successful in her dream-come-true business.

7. Believing in Yourself

If you don't believe in yourself, who will? It's been said that entrepreneurs are born leaders. You must be able to believe in yourself and your ability to accomplish your goal in order to motivate people to make things happen. They must believe in you and your product or service.

8. Taking Charge

After performing a feasibility report, many of Moldt's students found they did not want to be their own boss. The responsibilities of running a business can sometimes be too burdensome. Understand all the rules of the game and what is required to play. Know, also, what is required of a leader.

9. Recognizing Your Customer Is Always Number One

It is a lesson that baseball great Reggie Jackson taught Fields long ago. While the idea of being your own boss seems freeing, your are ultimately responsible to many people — the most important being your customer. Your customers will be judge and jury for your product or service. Whether you succeed or fail will depend a great deal on them.

10. Finding Your Support Group

Imagine individually creating 10,000 bars of soap by yourself. As Stacey Center can and will tell you, family was imperative to her success. Whether your support system is friends, family, or the entrepreneurial staff at Iowa State University, you must have a strong base. The more support you have from the business community, the greater your successes will be.

11. Acknowledging the Proverbial Village

What impact can a cookie, a mop, or a coffee shop have on local communities? Lane says that the real joy and sense of accomplishment from her business comes from what she's been able to give back at local, national, and global levels.

12. Knowing What Kind of Risks You're Willing to Take

Lane also says she would rather have tried to use her money — what little she had — to invest in her jewelry idea than to have asked, "What if?," for the rest of her life. I was in no condition to join the U.S. bobsled team so soon after having a baby, but if I had not tried, I would have wondered for the rest of my life about missed opportunities. Besides, if you turn failures into learning tools, you'll be ahead of the game.

Twelve Reasons You Should Not Start Your Own Business

Starting up your own business may not be for you. Sometimes, as a feasibility report might show, the risks are too great or, perhaps, a particular idea is not right for you. Experts agree there are definite red flags indicating when starting up a business is not right.

1. If Taking Risks Scares You

We take risks everyday. Some argue that we take risks by just getting out of bed every morning. However, if you are unwilling or unable to take pro-active risks that lead you beyond your normal, comfortable boundaries, entrepreneurialism is most likely not a tolerable risk for you.

When Tess Rano began her karate and kickboxing studio, she knew that, in order to bring more people to her, she would first have to go to them. Joining forces with a local charity, Rano held a kick-a-thon in a very busy parking lot to raise community spirit and awareness of her services. Just as Fields took to the street with cookies in hand, Rano put herself out in the public eye to be scrutinized — rejected or embraced. For both women, it was a scary move.

2. If You Lack the Knowledge or Skill

Passion is important, but it cannot be the only thing you have going for you. Cronbaugh investigated the coffee industry inside and out before she opened her doors, learning the different tastes and origins of each and every coffee bean.

Rano was involved in martial arts for more than two decades before taking on the role as chief instructor. To set yourself apart from your competitors, you must develop and hone the skills that in turn will sell your product or business. Also, if you want to succeed, you must be willing to put in long hours of research and planning even before you start your business — you must learn the rules of the game.

3. If You Require Structure

Total chaos is not a comfortable place to live. But in the business world, you are more apt to live in chaos than serenity. You must be willing and able to think fast on your feet. Also, you must be able to change direction quickly and easily while operating in an environment of uncertainty and semi-chaos.

4. If You Lack Self-Motivation

While owning your own business is certainly exciting, you must be honest with yourself. If the idea of free-falling, never knowing what the next day will bring, or having to do the brunt of the work yourself is more than you care to deal with, self-employment is an unwise choice. Also, if you need someone else to motivate you, self-employment is not for you.

Jeffrey A. Bernel, director of the Gigot Center for Entrepreneurial Studies at the University of Notre Dame says, "If you need the safety and assurances your business will succeed, hold on to your job and don't even think about starting your own business."

5. If You Are Doing It For Fun

While the idea of starting your own business may seem fun and exciting, a lot of blood, sweat, and tears must be put into the start-up. No successful business can be all fun and games.

6. If You Are Doing It For the Money

Often Fields asks what someone wants to do. Too many times they have no idea beyond wanting to strike it rich. As most businesswomen have told us, passion must be the main reason for going into business. If it is only money you seek, you will be disappointed and more likely to fail.

7. If You Just Want to Be Your Own Boss

Guess what? Your title may read CEO, but you will be answering to customers, vendors, suppliers, agents, and investors everyday.

8. If You Tend to Put Things Off

Remember Moldt's advice, "Always be ready to change with the market because the market is always changing." In today's business world, you must be able to think fast on your feet and be ready to modify your behavior. Some of the most damaging mistakes occur when management, afraid to move quickly, waits too long for more information. You must be able to meet deadlines and make decisions quickly, sometimes even with insufficient information.

9. If Ownership Is a Status Symbol

Coolidge of Gourmet Gifts warns that all too often we become more hung up on the title than actually being into the position — the work and the process. If it is a job title you seek, Coolidge suggests buying business cards for fun, thereby saving yourself a lot of headaches.

10. If Researching Your Idea Seems Too Much Trouble

You've got a great idea, so why not? Don't forget, seven out of every ten new businesses fail, so a lot of really good ideas have gone under. You must be sure your product or service is special.

11. If Family Pressure Is the Motivator

Often owners of a family business push their offspring into a business of their own. Elizabeth J. Gatewood, director of the Johnson Center for Entrepreneurship and Innovation at Indiana University in Bloomington says this is the wrong reason to go into business. "Do it because you really want to and you're prepared to dedicate yourself to the task of making it successful." The motivation and drive to start and develop your own business must come from within. It must be your passion, not someone else's.

12. If a SuperMom Complex Is the Motivator

The idea that you can work from home to simplify your life might be the greatest misconception of all. If you are an extremely organized person who easily greets and sets deadlines and handles multiple tasks, this could very well be for you. But, as Coolidge reminds us, too often home-based businesses are started with a faulty conception.

The Critical Question

To be or not to be, that is the question. Not one of the businesswomen I spoke with ever had a question as to whether she should do it. The twelve reasons to start a business were the modus operandi for these women. Each had a passion so strong, it could not be denied. But for women like Coolidge, the cost was ultimately too great.

The strain on and risk of destroying her marriage — because of the long hours she was devoting to her business — was too great. She knew what she wanted and weighed the cost. She sold Gourmet Gifts to future entrepreneur Lisa Nistico. But she had a great experience, came out on top, learned what was most important to her in life, and made a tidy little profit to boot.

With the announcement by the International Olympic Committee that women's bobsledding would be included in the 2002 Salt Lake City Games, there were just as many depressed people as there were elated ones. Some of the women knew that, had they held on a little longer, they could have been Olympians. I left on my own terms knowing I was a national champion. I slid on the World Cup circuit, garnered some great pictures and stories, and left with no regrets, no what-ifs.

Just as it is important to understand all the reasons for entering a new venture, it is equally important to understand when and why you should stay or move on.

When you enter the world of entrepreneurialism, be prepared for what is to come by believing in yourself, having the passion to sustain you, and being backed by family and friends.

Let there be few surprises.

Chapter 6

Breaking Down Boundaries

⌐

Imagine this scenario: "Hi, Dad. I've decided to drop out of medical school, but guess what? I made a nail polish color that matches my purse and sandals perfectly." Okay, maybe it didn't go exactly like that, but you can bet that folks at the Mohajer household were not happy when their daughter called with the news.

In fact, Dinch Mohajer did call her father to inform him she was quitting medical school, and she did believe she had found her calling — pastel nail polish colors. Admittedly, Mohajer had been unhappy in medical school for some time. Her interests were elsewhere. She had always had a creative flair but had not realized what her something special was until she needed a pale blue nail polish to match her sandals and purse. Frustrated there were no pastel colors other than pink on the market, Mohajer concocted the perfect blend from her own colors. When she began to get compliments from everyone around her, she realized she was on to something.

Once she had several sample colors to show, she gathered her courage and entered a chic boutique in Beverly Hills. While she was trying to make her sale with the manager of the store, a customer sashayed over, inspected the merchandise, and insisted on buying a bottle.

"Because I was mixing and pouring from my own room," says Mohajer, "they were pretty expensive." However, the customer was undeterred and bought a bottle for about twelve dollars.

That was the beginning of Hard Candies, Inc., and Mohajer's dive into the business world. Hard Candies, Inc. became a virtual overnight sensation, lining up clients such as Nordstrom, Sacs Fifth Avenue, Bloomingdale's, and Macy's. During the three years after that telephone call home, Mohajer has gone on to develop a multi-million dollar corporation and has been featured in fashion and celebrity magazines across the country. It was certainly a risk — medical school versus the cosmetic industry. But Mohajer saw the need and felt the passion. For her, becoming a risk-taker was the natural next step.

Certainly, women such as Mohajer are visionaries, but to make a niche for themselves in the business world, they must expose themselves to greater risks than are traditionally expected from women. It is not so easy to go against the basic training most women receive, but some people are natural risk-takers. Mohajer never second-guessed herself. Debbi Fields, who strutted into school every day wearing way-out clothes, marched to the beat of her own drum. Taking risks was part of who she was. She dared to be different.

Many people, particularly women, find the kind of scrutiny generated by expressed individuality difficult to handle. Daring to be different takes a firm belief in yourself. Even in these liberated times, women are generally not schooled or socially conditioned to be the kind of risk-taker who can stand up to criticism and nay-saying, affirming her position without being defensive. This makes female entrepreneurs all the more extraordinary.

Dr. Karen Stephenson, an anthropologist and a professor of management at the Anderson Graduate School of Management at UCLA, views taking risks as the only way to get ahead for women.

"The public rules are made by men for men," she explains. "When men move through societal structures, they are accustomed to seeing doors open for them. Even the most enlightened men can't understand what has never happened to them. They think if the door is opened for them, the door is opened for everyone. They simply cannot relate."

"Men are not trained to be risk-takers," she adds, "because they don't need to be. They are trained to work with one another, to form a network." They are, she points out, taught to work within a structure that was designed for them. Most men, for example, would never have put a payroll on their credit card as Krueger-Horn did. When Stephenson was asked if she considered herself a bit of a risk-taker, she could barely contain a snort. "A bit? Try a whole hell of a lot!"

Unexpected Boundaries

I had momentarily forgotten that this was the woman who was trudging across Guatemala, cutting her way through the rain forest, when she was held at gunpoint by guerrillas; the woman who set up her own corporation in just one week — in Norway. Stephenson in her late forties has been pushing back against, as she puts it, "the white glass ceiling," for most of her life.

Quite the opposite, I was in my late twenties (twenty-eight to be exact) before I even learned what the "good ol' boy network" was. A fact too embarrassing to admit to Stephenson. Truly, I'd been raised in a bubble world where everyone was treated equally or, at least, I thought so. There certainly didn't seem to be any restrictions for my sister or me.

My first experience to the contrary was with bobsledding. It was while the women struggled to get funding and sponsorship for sleds, equipment, uniforms, housing, food, and travel expenses from our own federation and the USOC that several of us learned all about the ol' boy network.

In case anyone out there is worried about it, the network is alive and thriving, thank you very much. After my own encounters, it came as no surprise to learn, while interviewing business leader after business leader, that these women had had many unpleasant experiences with the boys. While most of America has become more progressive as a society and most of us are busily knocking down stereotypes and biases, it seems the good ol' boys have drawn in their wagons and formed a much smaller but tighter circle.

In 1994, *Newsweek* magazine featured an article titled, "White, Male and Worried." The story detailed white men's concerns about the changing workplace demographics. "They recognize that they're still calling the shots and getting most of the promotions. But that does little to assuage fears that the pendulum will swing too far."[1]

Ninety-five percent of senior executives in this country are men. Of that group, ninety-seven percent are white males — a group, by the way, that makes up only forty-seven percent of the American workforce. But to listen to some of them talk, the best thing you could be is an African-

American woman. "They get all the breaks," is something heard all too often around the water cooler.

"Perhaps I am standing in the wrong line," Diane Jacobs laughed in response to that kind of thinking. Jacobs, an African-American woman, maintains that for all the grumbling and talk, "Unless you are a minority, you have no idea how we've struggled."

Although she came up with the name and concept of The Cakeworks, funded the money for start-up costs and ran the show, her white, male partner was seen as the man in charge. "Because my partner was white," Jacobs recalls, "people always assumed that he owned the place. People would look right through me. They were deferring to my partner over me because they wanted to talk to a white man. He had no idea until I finally pulled

This all-cake and icing basket of fruit , flowers, and champagne, one of Jacob's specialties, exhibits her fine artistic, baking, and frosting, talents; and it tastes as good as it looks

him aside and explained how hurtful this kind of thinking can be. I was not even getting the credit for my own work, my own ideas.

"I don't know. Maybe I need to go stand in the African-American-women-getting-all-the-breaks line, because I'm sure not catching them right now." Is there anyone who thinks the Whoopi Goldberg movie, *The Associate*, is not a reflection of real life?

According to a recent study conducted by the Women's Business Enterprise National Council (WBENC), Uncle Sam may not be as supportive of minorities and women as we would hope. In 1996, only one and one-half percent of federal monies went to women-owned businesses, despite the government's goal of providing at least five percent of contract dollars to entrepreneurial women. In fact, only three of the thirteen federal agencies responsible for federal contract dollars met the five percent goal for women. And, as the preceding pages have demonstrated, obtaining loans from banks is not any easier for women entrepreneurs.

Fields secured a loan fairly quickly, but she was lucky. Her husband has a reputation in the business world, and the bank was willing to make a loan strictly on good faith — in him. Krueger-Horn was not so lucky. She had a difficult time convincing banks that people would buy her cookies. So if the banks wouldn't go for cookies, how do you think they felt about bathtub stoppers as necklaces? Jenai Lane was bounced right out of the banks. Entrepreneurs Helen Yee and Diane Slater used stocks from their employers as collateral for a loan when they decided to open the first massage clinic in their state. Mary Kay Ash cashed in her life savings. Only now does Cozy Wolan of Cozy's Cuts for Kids laugh about going to just about every bank in New York City. It was a very depressing and difficult time for her. If she hadn't had passion, sheer will, and determination, there were times it would have been easy to abandon the idea altogether.

Going to a bank was not even an option for Lynette Reed. What bank would loan money to an unemployed ex-model so she could make candles? She had no choice but to sell all her belongings to fund her start-up costs. Eloise Blackmon borrowed money from her sister to lease minivans. Gretchen Leddy and her husband, Bernie, did try the bank route but found the banks' conditions extremely unappealing.

"The banks were not flexible at all," Leddy says. "All my life I wanted to be in business for myself; but if we had taken a loan from the banks, we would have been working for them. They told us we would have to show our assets at certain times; and they could pull our loan at any time, just say it was due. If we had gone with a bank loan, we might not have our business today because we had a few really lean years. We literally lived off of credit cards."

So how did they do it? They turned to family. "We obtained a small loan through the family. We're still paying it back." But they are doing it on their terms. The team effort paid off. Bachman's Bakery has been turning a nice profit for the Leddys and has a secure fixture in the Columbus, Ohio, community.

Jennifer Maxwell, creator of PowerBar, avoided the banks as well. What bank would have considered a twenty-year-old college student and a thirty-two-year-old marathon runner living on an $8,000-a-year coach's salary as a low enough risk? Instead, the Maxwells used the money that Brian made during his Olympic marathon days — specifically, $50,000 from an appearance in a Xerox advertisement — as their financial backing. Still, there were risks. If their bars had not sold, their life savings would have disappeared. "We were bold. We were very sure of what we were doing," Maxwell says.

Jennifer Maxwell formulating a new PowerBar recipe

It took all of their money to produce 30,000 bars, with no money left over for marketing or advertisements. Instead, they began attending marathons, handing out the bars to runners. "We thought if they [the runners] could have a bar in hand, they'd use it and like it; there could be no better marketing."

Targeting a variety of races, the Maxwells and PowerBar soon became a well-known and much sought after part of the racing world. Be creative. There are numerous ways to bypass relying on banks. Your support foundation — which is usually made up of family — is often the most helpful. One budding entrepreneur wrote letters to several family members with an attached contract stating that whatever she borrowed, whatever they were able to loan, she would repay with two percent interest. The family — her team — loved the idea of a group effort. Long lost aunts, uncles, godparents, and cousins all joined in. Now a newsletter updates the family on the progress of her invention, from obtaining a patent and creating a prototype to its manufacture and introduction into the marketplace.

You needn't give up on banks entirely. Diane Jacobs of The Cakeworks in Los Angeles followed a formula very close to Fields'. After writing

her own business proposal, she took it to investors to get start-up capital. Her family and friends did kick in one-third of the start-up fees to
secure a Small Business Administration (SBA) loan. But the SBA office
advised her that they don't lend money, they guarantee it. "So they referred me to Pacific Coast Regional, a development corporation that
makes state guaranteed SBA loans."

Entering the world of high finance is, indeed, a dizzying experience.
Remember those weed-out classes you were forced to take your fresh-
man year, where 200 people were packed into one room? This is the
same weed-out principal. Only those who really, really want a loan keep
coming back for more.

Bank executive Vanessa Freytag explains that banks really do want to
lend you money. "The good banks will sit down with you and tell you
what they want. You might have the information but did not include it.
You might not know what the bank is looking for. It is still a mystery,"
she laughs. "Each bank wants something different. A bank may say *no*
due to lack of information. Once you understand what they want, you
may be able to regroup and come back in another two to six months
with what they want."

Yee and Slater were also aggressive with the banks and were rewarded.
In fact, Slater jokes that they couldn't miss with their combined background — Yee has a fine arts degree and Slater an engineering degree.

Slater's and Yee's new building for Massage Away, and their school

They're what Ed Moldt regards as a perfect combination for success: they "have the creative vision of an artist and the technical, practical sense of a businessperson."

When their massage clinic took off and needed expanding, Yee and Slater turned to the banks once again. "Every three years we made a bid to various banks. We would say, This is what we did and if you are interested we would like to meet with you and see what you have to offer us. Usually, we would get about eight responses. We would meet over massage tables; forget meeting over boardroom tables. They would see our clients in the waiting room and get a feel for who we were. We gave a pitch, and they would give us a pitch back."

Another interesting advantage for using the banks, as far as Slater and Yee are concerned, is that it eased the tricky relationships between friendship and business partner. Because the partners had to answer to the bank, it took some of the strain away from the personal aspect of being partners. "It formalized the risks," says Slater. "The bank really defined a lot of things instead of owing [money to] each other. Everything was in writing through the bank." The strain of business and money on personal relationships can take a toll on even the most determined and loving friends and family.

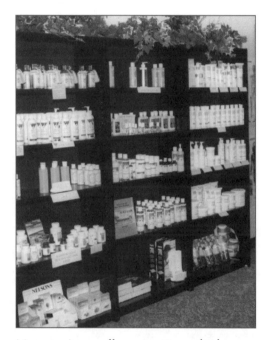

Massage Away offers massage and relaxation products to its clients and customers

As for Jacobs, she was going it alone, fighting the powerful banking system. But she stuck with it, creating and recreating business plans until she met with a loan officer from Pacific Coast Bank. At that point, her business plan and experience in her field came into play. She talked to him about her business plan, her vision, and past experience as a cake

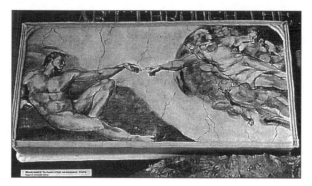

Inspired by Michelangelo's Sistine Chapel ceiling, a second masterpiece by Diane Jacobs

decorator (eight years to be exact), and he was sold. But it had not been an easy ride. Despite her cake decorating experience, Jacobs had no business experience, which posed a problem for a half dozen banks before Pacific Coast.

Moldt explains that you cannot expect banks to lend you money until you understand how, when, and why banks are able to make money available. Freytag agrees. "A lot of times entrepreneurs want to tell me all about their product or company," she says, "they are so excited about it. But they really haven't gone through the numbers. They haven't told me anything about the finances or the projections for the company or personal data.

"What is the first thing you want to know when you lend someone money?" she postulates. "You want to know when they are going to pay you back. Banks are no different. We need to know you can pay us back." Jacobs, Yee, and Slater understood this and presented themselves accordingly.

There are still more opportunities to be found outside the banking community, as Tara Cronbaugh learned. Like Jacobs, Yee, and Slater, Cronbaugh found a business proposal to be crucial for getting her foot in the door. As a twenty-year-old college student whose only experience in business was the successful completion of half of a sixteen-week entrepreneurial course at the University at Iowa, she didn't exactly create a comfortable feeling with local bankers.

When she began to formulate her idea of opening a coffee house, she didn't even like the taste of coffee. But she researched and wrote a business proposal. She talked to coffee house managers and owners to get a better feel for how to present her case. "I wrote the business plan for the class, and the professor gave me pointers," Cronbaugh recalls. Then she went to the Small Business Development Center on campus. "They suggested I go through the Iowa state-funded program called Target Small Business Bureau." That was the beginning for Cronbaugh and her Iowa City Coffee Company.

It is unfortunate many women have no idea what is out there or how to get in touch with organizations set up to assist entrepreneurial women. Learning about and using the resources available to you, such as the ones mentioned in this book, are musts if you want to succeed. Perhaps, as more women learn about business and how these resources can help them, there will be more women motivated to become successful entrepreneurs.

WBENC is a new nonprofit consortium of major corporations formed to provide women with their own support group. "The goal of the program is to enhance opportunities for women to do business with major corporations and government bodies," says Susan Bari, executive director of WBENC.[2] Likewise, Count-Me-In.org. is dedicated to giving economic power to women entrepreneurs. These kinds of wonderful resources create more opportunities and successes for women in business. The idea is to unite and empower women, so they no longer have to face the good ol' boy network alone.

Kleinkauf on an outing holds a coho salmon

Kleinkauf was never one to back away from a challenge. After all, she says, she has had to work and be competitive in a man's world. But when she crossed over to the all-male domain of flyfishing, she and others were in for a surprise.

"I'll never forget it. It was an early trip when we got started. I had several women with me when this fellow came over to us and said, 'You women get off this river. This is our river.' Our river!?

I knew that guiding was a man's business, but I had never been so confronted. We were all sort of taken aback. We all stood there in stunned silence for a moment, and then, boy, that poor fellow. We really let him have it."

Since those early days on the river, Kleinkauf has set up the first-ever women's website on flyfishing, has been invited by mega-flyfishing companies Ross Reels, Mustad Hooks, and Patagonia to serve as a professional guide, and continues to be an outstanding and respected member of the International Flyfishing Association. "There are," Kleinkauf points out, "no boundaries in the great outdoors."

No Boundaries

It is interesting how many of the women I interviewed avoided the word boundaries. Oh, they exist. No one disputed that. Yet, for women like Wolan, Fields, Jenny Craig and Jennifer Floren, the word did not exist in their world. "Define your own rules," Floren says. "Now more than ever we have the freedom to define new parameters for building our careers."

Instead of defining parameters, Fields likened the business world to sports, noting the importance of learning the rules of the game to be a better player and have more fun. But what Fields really did was design her own game. It was a game with rules, you can be sure. There was a standard of excellence and quality she always expected of herself and her employees, but there were never any boundaries. "In sports, I have always been open-minded, ready to try something new and to work hard. This is the way I approached business as well. It is the only way to learn something new and to succeed."

Perhaps this is why Fields wouldn't take *no* for an answer when she was told the chewy cookie concept would never fly. The good 'ol boy network does exist, but forewarned is forearmed, as my dad always says. Successful business people work around obstacles, and successful businesswomen learn to work around the limitations and rules of the game established by the boys.

You can create your own game and rules. In a national survey, Deborah Swiss, author of *Women Breaking Through: Overcoming the Final 10 Obstacles at Work*, found that women believe there is a gender bias in the business world and that breaking the rules is the only way to get ahead. However, instead of breaking those rules, women business leaders suggest redefining the game plan. When you can define what your game is, you have a better chance of designing a business strategy that works for you.

The Name of the Game

If you don't like the game, change it. Sharon Leone, CEO of Sweet Favors, for example, did just that. She had earned the name Candy Girl in college because of her love of candy and the unbridled enthusiasm she had for the candy shop she worked in. After college, she worked full-time for the candy shop. Several times she tried to buy the business from the current owners who also owned forty other businesses. Her hope was that something could be arranged with the owners, especially since she was already working in the business. A budding entrepreneur, she tried to entice them with the idea of opening up candy stores under their name on college campuses around the nation, but they told her they'd rather kill the business than sell.

Leone did not have the option of obtaining a loan from a bank. As a young woman with no collateral and very little experience in the business world — never mind she had worked in the very store she hoped to buy — banks considered her too great a risk. So she changed the game plan, deciding to work from home selling candy to corporations rather than to individuals. However, she knew nothing of corporate accounts, premiums, and ad specialties.

Now, Leone laughs about the hand-drawn designs for logos she sent to companies as samples. She says at the time she had no idea they were so bad. She had no experience in marketing and had done little research about how to make presentations. Now, she shutters. As Fields says, presentation is everything. Leone began to figure that out as more doors closed. She reassessed and adopted Fields' way of thinking.

She needed to learn the rules. If she was going to make a go of it, she would have to learn what the rules and the penalties were. She began talking to business professors at the University of California, realtors, and owners of private businesses about putting company logos on candies. If she didn't know about a company, she researched and began refining her marketing skills. What did they want? How was this company different from that one?

Remember the all-important feasibility study? Leone was on the right track by reevaluating her idea. She was able to modify her thinking and, instead of buying into a business in an already established property, Leone created her own work environment at home. She had extremely low overhead costs, which Moldt recommends. However, she had not really tested her market, so she spent more time and energy learning from her mistakes because she still did not understand the rules.

Her big break came when VISA gave her an order for 62,500 embossed chocolate coins. A net of $16,000. Still working from her house, her team came into play once again. She used some of the proceeds to buy an embossing machine and called on her parents, five brothers, and one sister for help. In three weeks, the family embossed, individually wrapped, and shipped the coins. Sales took off from there. Within two years she moved out of her house and doubled her work space.

Like Leddy, Leone recognizes that the first few years consisted of long, hard hours, but they were hers. "I could have easily quit," she says, just as Leddy could have during those lean years. Instead, Leone remained focused and committed to the game, creating a secure, successful business for herself and her new and growing family.[3]

Redefining the Game

There are many examples of how women have managed to nurture an idea into a dream come true. Family, financial institutions, networking, and a sprinkle of good luck all played a large part in moving their projects forward. Perhaps, you're asking yourself:

- Where do I start?
- What is a mission statement?
- How do I start a feasibility study?
- What is a business proposal, or plan?
- How do I know if I am on the right track?

No one can tell you, precisely, how to make it work. As one consultant so eloquently put it, if he could tell us all how to run our businesses, he would be running them rather than being a career counselor. Each business is unique to its owner, and each owner has her or his own style that contributes to its success. However, doing extensive research and following your own sense of style is the beginning.

A common theme of business leaders in this book is the importance of passion. From passion, great ideas are born. With passion, rules can be changed. Once you have discovered what your passion is, anything goes. Yes, there were already cookies on the market. But no one said you couldn't make an oversized chewy cookie — well, actually they did, and Mrs. Fields proved them wrong. There were pick-me-up snacks on the market, but no one had ever seen anything like the Powerbar before. And, certainly, there were coffee houses long before Tara Cronbaugh came along.

Cronbaugh developed the idea of a cozy coffee house long before the set of "Friends" filled millions of living rooms around the globe. Because her location was a college setting, Cronbaugh envisioned more comfortable and elegant furnishings from local antique shops as a home-away-from-home feel for her clientele. With plenty of chess, checkers, and backgammon games, over twenty-five magazines, and seven daily newspapers in stock, this would be the place to come. She even encouraged local artists by using her walls as their gallery. It became a community center of sorts. That was the Tara Touch. Then, from all her research and interviews with similar businesses, Cronbaugh determined what supplies she needed and how much to order.

Without making it more difficult that need be, there are a few questions you should ask yourself before you begin any business venture. Remember how often Fields would ask someone what it was they wanted to do with their lives and found they didn't know. Now is your chance to answer some important questions.

Moldt asks his students to consider:

- Where you are presently?
- What does your future hold?
- If you perceive you have boundaries, how you define them?

If you can't answer these questions effectively, you can't possibly adhere to the rules of the game. How can you write a mission statement or know if you are on the right track if you don't know what you would most like to do with your life? If you can't answer the question of where you are in your life right now or what the personal risks might be for you, how can you know if you are creating an accurate business proposal? First and foremost, remember this:

Without passion, there is no game.

Michael Jordan forever changed the game of basketball because of the kind of passion he brought to the courts. During the 2000 Olympic games, the U.S. women's soccer team once again captured our hearts — and the silver medal — with their undaunting spirit, determination, drive, and overwhelming passion for the game and each other.

As is true of many of the women in this book, Fields was able to nurture her idea into a thriving business because of a deep, personal passion for her product, herself, and what she was doing. This game is yours to play if you have the passion.

To understand the basics of this game you need to be able to answer the following questions.

The Timeless Ten

1. What would you most like to do with your life?
2. Where are you now?
3. How can you achieve your goal?
4. What is your time frame?
5. What kind of networking system do you have?
6. How can you gain access to more relevant information?
7. What are the costs?
8. What are the risks?
9. What is the pay-off?
10. Who wants or needs your product or service?

You really can't answer most of the questions, however, until you have answered the last one — until you understand your market. Again, that means, research.

Bear with me on this analogy. I've been forced to watch *Chitti Chitti Bang Bang* with my five- and seven-year-olds for the umpteenth time, so I'll use the mad professor's Toot Sweet Candy Treat as an example. Let's say that you have just invented the Toot Sweet Candy Treat that goes toot when you tweet it. You think it is a marvelous contraption. Not only does it taste wonderful, not only is it a treat that lasts all day, but it toots when you tweet it.

First you must ask yourself, are there any other tooting treats on the market? Is this something completely new? And, if so, is the cost of manufacture reasonable? Can you afford to mass produce it? If there are similar tooting treats on the market, what could be the spin on this one? Maybe the others only have one toot pitch where yours can actually play songs. Maybe a miniature song book could be included with the treat. Maybe, because of its unique design, children could easily carry it around their neck on a string or wear it like a ring. Perhaps an adult version could be produced with a favorite alcoholic beverage as a fun holiday party favor. You get the idea.

Understanding the market place and the market value of your toot treat is imperative to finding your niche. Then you can move forward with the other questions:

- How will I produce it?
- Where can I produce it?
- How will I market it?
- What will the initial start-up costs be?
- Who will my target audience (market) be?

Only when you've answered these questions, will you be ready to talk seriously with investors — regardless of whether they are friends, family, or banks. It's important to remember, just because friends and family are friends and family, you still want to treat them as team players. You must help them understand the rules and be certain they know the penalties.

In order to obtain the information you need, to answer the above and other questions, you must launch two projects:

- Conduct a feasibility study
- Begin writing your business plan

Understanding Your Market

The chapter opened with Dineh Mohajer, founder of Hard Candies, Inc. Mohajer created a fun, ultra-hip line of nail polish colors for today's trendy youth. Sales took off as Mohajer established outstanding contracts with Nordstrom, Bloomingdale's, and Macy's. By young consumer standards, however, Hard Candies is an expensive product. Good, but expensive. Enter Kristin Penta and Fun cosmetics.

Penta moved in, filling a void for the teen market. According to the consumer research company Teenage Research Unlimited, a typical teenager spends an average of $89 per week on clothing, jewelry, beauty, and entertainment. What Penta discovered was that if Fun Cosmetics could create fun, exciting, and affordable cosmetics, it could establish a loyal customer base. By doing so, she has been dubbed the Martha Stewart of the teen world, appearing on daytime talk shows and on regional and national news programs, including CNN, as a trend spotter.

By understanding her market, Penta was able to create a company, effectively market it and herself, and establish herself as the foremost expert in teen fashion.

"We call it cheap chic," Penta laughs. "I felt there was a need out there." The need, as Penta describes it, is also for today's youth — the youth who have limited budgets. "I wanted something really convenient. A bike ride away with not a lot of financial commitment." Penta, twenty-eight, remembers how it was when she was a kid.

"I grew up in suburbia. Everything I saw was really expensive. My mom would have to drive me to the stores and buy me what I wanted, which was usually only for the prom." By creating Fun Cosmetics, Penta ensured that just about every hip-hop kid in America could go to her or his local Walgreens or CVS for inexpensive, washable body ink, lip gloss, color glitter sticks, and fruity nail enamel. In short, Penta was quick to figure out that, while the department stores have the prestige, the discount stores are where the action is.

"You think of the department stores as the epitome of the best," says Penta, "but they only have 100 stores each. Whereas, someplace like Walmart has 4,000 stores. That's where the money is." Before the first glitter lip gloss hit the assembly line, Penta knew who her target audience was and understood manufacturing costs, mark ups, and what was needed to turn a profit.

Understanding your market — to be discussed further in the next chapter — is the key to your success. In 1997, teenage girls spent $43.5 billion on retail items — more than any other consumer group. Understanding this demographic literally put Fun Cosmetics and Penta on the map. The business map.

In fact, Penta did everything by the book. So when it came to the end of the interview and I asked, as always, what would she do over if she had the chance, Penta was hard-pressed. Finally she relented, "I would paint my whole office purple and make everyone wear glitter sunglasses in the hallways."

Make that rose-colored glitter sunglasses?

Chapter 7

Establishing Your Image

⌇

One of the most brilliant snack ideas on the U.S. market came in 1997 when Nestlé introduced the chocolate-covered pretzel in miniature packets. The packets could be found beside the candy in grocery store check-out isles. It was inspired. Let's face it, who does the shopping? Women. And what do they crave? Chocolate. In particular, when certain cycles in our lives occur, what are the two things women reportedly crave the most? Salty things such as french fries and pretzels, and sweets, especially chocolate. For Nestlé to have combined the two and stuck the little packages up with the candy — for all menstruating women to see — was a stroke of sheer genius.

In fact, the only way they goofed was not to have made commercials touching lightly and humorously on this very subject. Every female consumer would have been amused and appreciative that this company understood their wants and needs.

Despite that marketing oversight, each time I was at the store I would usually throw a couple of bags onto the pile of groceries. I waited for the test-pilot stage to be over with. I waited for Nestlé to decide there really was a market for this product and come out with bigger sized bags. And I waited.

By the end of the summer I even called their 800 number on the back of the package. Because I was pregnant at the time — another big chocolate and salt craving stage in a woman's life — I might have been a little more aggressive than I needed to be. But I had to ask, "Is this some sort of toy you're selling? Where's the real deal?" I couldn't believe that this was all they were going to do. But it was. Unmoved by my hormonal pleas and presumably unaware of the actual market, no larger bags were produced.

Then, in the beginning of 1999, I noticed a new company had stepped in to fill the void. Snyders of Hanover, an old, well-established pretzel manufacturer, began selling larger bags at double the price. I bought two bags. Finally, Nestlé started selling a larger bag.

The lesson here is simple and basic: no matter how good the product, it can always be improved. In this case, it was merely the size of the packaging. In the case of Mrs. Fields' Cookies, a nation's preference for the traditional, crispy cookie was converted to a love of the soft, chewy cookie. Like Nestlé, Fields learned that no matter how fabulous the notion, the idea, the product, the cookie, first you must find a way to promote it. Success cannot come until you generate some interest. Fields had done virtually no advertising or marketing for her cookies. She was sure of just one thing: "People love my cookies." But that wasn't enough. It was not until she physically went out onto the streets — and all but force-fed passers-by — that word about her great cookies got out.

Market Yourself and Your Business

There is a cab driver who lives down the street from where I live. As near as I can tell, his is a family-owned business. As someone who loves and supports small businesses, I would love to give him my business. On the rare occasions that I have been in need of a ride to the airport or have had some transportation problem, it would have been great to call on a cab just down the street from me. He would know just where I lived. I wouldn't have to wait around forever, hoping the cab would get me to the airport on time. But there is one problem. It's the bumper sticker on the back of his cab. It reads:

There's a Party in My Pants
And Everyone is Coming!

Now I ask you. Would you want to get into a vehicle with a guy who thought the saying was so clever he felt compelled to display it as part of his business advertisement? You want to find a strategy that makes you different and memorable, but you don't want to be remembered for having a party in your pants.

Hard work alone won't get potential customers to buy your product or service. You must learn to blow your own horn. No one else is going to do it for you. This is a difficult concept for women, in particular, after so many years of training to be humble and self-effacing. Only men are allowed bragging rights. Right? Wrong! As an entrepreneur, you will have to make phone calls on your own behalf, raving about your product. You will have to write press releases and contact the press about your grand opening, prepare reviews of your own service or product, and write advertising copy.

Gretchen Leddy chooses to use small community papers to advertise because "people like to support small business." Her bakery initially did a lot of bridal shows, using these events to show off her beautiful craftsmanship. In her case, relying on support from the community worked. But you may find, if you are in a larger city or are trying to appeal to a mass audience, you need something beyond local papers and community spirit.

In 1982, Nancy Brinker founded the Komen Foundation for breast cancer survivors. It was, however, around the same time the Vietnam War Memorial was being erected in Washington, D.C. It was all everyone was talking about. While Brinker herself appreciated the importance of the memorial, she spun her own word campaign to get the message out about the Komen Foundation. It packed a powerful wallop that no one could ignore. "In a ten-year period, 58,000 lives were lost in Vietnam. In the same ten-year period, 330,000 women died of breast cancer. But there is no wall dedicated to them."[1]

PowerBar became a household name in the sporting world when U.S. cyclists in the 1987 Tour de France showed off their PowerBars on television. Suddenly, everyone wanted to know what the Americans were carrying. The other athletes usually ate ham and cheese — a cumbersome and sometimes messy pick-me-up. The neatly packaged, low-fat, high-carb energy bars were ideal for the athletes and suddenly, "After the Tour de France, we couldn't make them [the bars] fast enough," says Jennifer Maxwell. The Maxwells' marketing plan hung on an assumption that turned out to be correct. By giving free bars during an international event to leaders of one of their core markets, their value would be spread quickly by word of mouth.

"Pudge" Kleinkauf had to be much more proactive. She couldn't exactly hang out at her local stream and wait for a lost band of flyfishers to happen by. "This was a very important part of the business," says Kleinkauf. "There wasn't a pool of women to talk to because they didn't even know they could flyfish. First, I created a mailing list. I went to a computer company, the same that a lot of politicians use, and had them compile a list of women who had bought a fishing license in the past year. I did direct mail to them and told them who I was, what I was doing, and that classes were available. I still use that list today, always updating and refining it.

"Next, I put together a professional brochure. Then I began calling women's groups. I asked if they were looking for women speakers for anything. Many times there were political or business functions looking for speakers." Kleinkauf couldn't wait for word of mouth and generated her own energy on the Internet. The name of her home page is simple, to the point, and easily found by any search engine: *Women's Flyfishing®*. Also you can go to it directly at *www.halcyon.com/wffn/* (women's flyfishing network).

Jennifer Floren also used the Internet to draw in a strong customer base. Promising anxious twenty-somethings advice, guidance, and the insight of thousands of recent graduates, *www.experience.com* has been getting more than a million hits per month. Her strategy was nothing short of brilliant. Floren knew that by getting millions of hits, companies and universities would line up to be part of this young professional graduate market. She was right.

"experience.com, a nationwide membership organization for young professionals, is used by more than 130 universities nationwide. We have

Jennifer Floren

set out to make the life of a young professional easier." She has succeeded. And at the tender age of twenty-seven, Floren was named by
Working Woman magazine as part of the "Power Pack" to watch out for.

Respect, Inc. hit the big time when Jenai Lane developed a nail polish that is heat sensitive, changing colors according to the wearer's
mood. The nail polish, called P.M.S. (Polish Mood Shades) landed Lane
on several talk shows, including the Rosie O'Donnell Show, and got her
featured in magazines and
newspapers around the country. But, to her surprise, the
brand name was considered
offensive by some and received
criticism. Bottles were even
pulled from the shelves in a
Minneapolis store. However,
it was exactly this kind of
scandal that brought notori-
ety to the company. Because
Lane believed in her product,
she developed a sense of humor about the negative response. When she appeared
on the Howard Stern show,
the famous shock jock asked

Lane and Rosie O'Donnell show off P.M.S.

her if there was a color called Bitch. Her answer: "No. We're too busy
working on the shade, Living with an Ass."

"When I first thought of P.M.S.," says Lane, "I thought, 'No, this is
much too irreverent. I'll never get away with this.' But you know what?
I'm really about risks. This could be a great political statement. Women
are not allowed to talk about this. Whenever a woman is focused or aggressive, she is called a bitch. I wanted to take all the negative names
when women are P.M.S.-ing and restructure the stereotypes."

Although Lane did not anticipate the negative reactions, she stands
by the name and the product. She is single-handedly trying to dispel
negative stereotypes, and sales continue to climb.

Whatever your feelings are about the name P.M.S., you have to ap-
plaud the name of the actual company, Respect, Inc. Even the company

logo is an innovative eye-catcher that leaves people talking. Lane chose a thumbprint because, she says, "When you look at someone's thumbprint, you can't tell whether they are a man or a woman, black or white, rich or poor. You can't judge someone on those attributes. Everyone is deserving of respect."

Bravo. It is a marketing campaign deserving of respect, and certainly one you can't forget.

Market Your Image and Target Your Customers

In an age of more — more advertisements, more competition, more Internet, more everything — the only way to be successful and stand out is to find your target audience and sell yourself or your product (often one and the same) by creating a new and exciting energy. The customer must feel a part of that new and exciting something.

As owner of the East Coast Ernie Reyes School of Karate, selling motivation is crucial to Tess Rano's success as a karate and kick-boxing instructor. Riding the tide of the popularity created by Billy Blanks and his Tae Bo Aerobics, Rano acts as part drill sergeant, part best friend, part entertainer to keep the energy level in her classes high and the client return rate even higher.

"It's my job to make this a positive place. A lot of the women here don't want to go to gyms because of all the beautiful people. They feel insecure about that. The energy here is a lot more positive. We're friends, working together. And as hard as they are working, I am, too. They like to think I'm suffering with them."

Generating that kind of feeling isn't exclusive to customer service. J'Amy Owens, president of The Retail Group, Inc. in Seattle, Washington, maintains that a feeling can be generated by a product as well.[2] Other businesswomen agree and offer some valuable tips on how to create an audience grabber through effective marketing.

Inclusion

One of the most sought after consultants in the retail business, with customers the like of Starbucks, Blockbuster, and NIKE, Owens regards Gap, Inc. as the most successful retailer in America because it sells inclusion, offering the customer a sense of belonging. "The Gap is selling us not a T-shirt but membership in a club," she says. The Gap has also turned one of its holdings, Banana Republic, into "the department store for Generation Y." In addition, its discount outlet, Old Navy, "has figured out how to sell value in a way that is not demeaning or belittling," as is the case with most other discount stores. Similarly, at Westerville's Ernie Reyes School of Karate, there is a real sense of inclusion for the participants. They are not just getting a work-out and paying for a service, they are part of the club.

Trust

At Annie's Edibles, the service goes far beyond providing quality food. "I'm here for support as well," says owner Annalisa Mastroianni. "I have clients who call, saying, 'I'm at a restaurant. I don't have your food. What should I eat?' Our clients are like family. I know who's in town, who's not."

Mastroianni believes that her company — or any company for that matter — must give customers what they want before the business can be successful. Serving the customers' needs is the only way to build trust. Owens agrees, "It is this kind of trust factor that creates a very strong, loyal customer backing."

Blockbuster Video was built upon this factor of trust. Blockbuster does not rent or sell movies that are different from other video rental companies, but the name Blockbuster has become one consumers know and trust. Their slogan, "Make it a Blockbuster night," is something many households do because they can depend on a quality selection.

Customer service, Mastroianni says, is about "a relationship between business and customer."

Higher Purpose

When Lane created Respect, Inc., one of the things she most wanted to sell, beyond the actual products, was the idea of respect itself. She started with the company logo — the thumbprint. "Each thumbprint is like a snowflake. It is unique. There are no two alike. I thought what a great place this would be without all the racism and sexism."

Respect, Inc. is a socially-conscious business that has dedicated itself to such causes as battered women and children, AIDS, cancer, and endangered species. It is Lane's thumbprint on the world — hoping to make a difference — and her customers are invited to take a stand with her. Knowing they are connected to a company committed to fighting intolerance, poverty, and hopelessness, customers can feel good about the purchases they make.

Get Your Name on Everyone's Lips

Lane got what she was after in more ways than one. By producing hip new products, her jewelry and accessories are all the rage with Generation X consumers — a powerful group. By stirring up her own bit of controversy, whether intentional or not, the name of Respect, Inc. and Jenai Lane became mutually hot topics.

Because of the nature of their businesses, Cheryl Krueger-Horn, Debbi Fields, Gretchen Leddy, and Tara Cronbaugh capitalized on location as their primary advertisement. They counted on being in good locations and providing quality products as sufficient to bring in new clientele and repeat customers.

A mixture of luck and craft can be the greatest source of advertising, as Lynette Reed and Diane Jacobs will attest. While both women are exceedingly gifted in what they do, both were fortunate to have celebrity patrons who quickly spread the word about their businesses.

As much as Jacobs loves decorating cakes, her real passion is screen writing. Once she designed a cake for Steven Spielberg and added a little surprise — baked, decorated, and presented alongside the cake was one of her scripts. The plan didn't work, but who knows what might happen with her next creative marketing venture. In the meantime, she has no intentions to quit her day job.

During her grand opening, Mrs. Fields was forced to leave her post to peddle her cookies on the street. B. Smith worked the rounds in her Manhattan restaurant every night. "Day and night I was in the restaurant. I walked around to every table, talked to every person who came in. That's how I built my business." Like Fields, Smith used her name as a brand. It was a product that she stood by, and it is the foundation of her marketing campaign.[3]

Risk reduction is certainly an essential planning goal, but learning to take self-promotional risks such as these is equally important.

Of course, impressing your name on the minds of other people is not always about location or physical products. Take Cris Dolan, for example. As president of *OneMain.com* (your hometown Internet) in New York City, Dolan is one of the most sought-after troubleshooters in the nation. She's been courted by all the major networks, Hearst Multimedia (the largest media conglomerate in the United States), and Microsoft — by CEO Bill Gates.

Dolan was a pioneer in developing advanced technology businesses and products, including Internet, wireless, eCommerce, interactive television, executive information systems, and communications and network management technologies. While studying for her masters of science degree at MIT's prestigious Media Lab, Dolan was a research assistant in the News in the Future research consortium. She worked on the early prototypes for interactive information and entertainment. As a founder of *OneMain.com*, one of the ten largest Internet service providers, she conceived and launched OneMain's Geographic Communities. These web portals provide local information and communications as a tool to develop revenue streams, strengthen customer relationships, build brand loyalty, and increase customer retention for smaller metropolitan and rural markets.

There is no question that Dolan is a risk-taker. Not only was she one of the first women to compete internationally in the sport of skeleton, she was ranked worldwide. For those who aren't familiar with this insane sport, the athlete lies on his or her stomach on a seventy-pound steel sled and speeds face first down a mountain.

Cris Dolan off to a flying start in the 1994 World Cup Championship races in Germany. She won the gold

Fortunately, business does not require that kind of risk-taking in order to be successful. But it's not the physical dare-devil stunts that separates Dolan from the pack, it's her attitude. In business, Dolan exemplifies Ed Moldt's philosophy: she invests little or no money of her own. Also, she's the perfect Moldt model for one who thinks fast on her feet, is able to modify her behavior quickly and efficiently, and is aware of her market value.

It is Dolan's behavior that many consider cutting-edge. Recently, she was called by a headhunter who informed her that a huge, international, multi-media group wanted her expertise. Although Dolan was happy where she was, she is not one to turn down an opportunity blindly, even though it required traveling to a different country for the interview. She was curious, "Just to see what they had to say." However, her interviewers quickly found out that Dolan had come to interview them. She asked, "Why should I come to work for you?" They wanted to hire her immediately, but *they* didn't pass *her* test.

In the world of business and technology, Dolan stands out. She brings more than just brains to the marketing table. She knows her stuff, and she knows she's the best at what she does. This kind of understanding and appreciation of one's self-worth is important to the health, happiness, and reputation of any businessperson. Dolan understands this and provides a successful and healthy role model for women.

In a discussion about brand name products, a real estate agent once asked Owens of The Retail Group if it is possible to *brand* a person. As we have discussed, promoting an actual product seems easier than promoting one's self. Owens response: "Let me tell you something, U-DA-BRAND. Start marketing. Do things that no one else dares to do."

Like Dolan, Owens believes that a brand or name can be product or person. Success can be limitless. It is how you sell yourself (or the product) that will stick in the minds of the consumer. As all the businesswomen I have talked with have stated, it is important to identify what your strengths are, then market them. Is it your ability to work with others? Your creative sense of style? Or, perhaps, it's your ability to conceptualize and organize or to design fabulous jewelry.

It is equally important to figure out what your weaknesses are and seek council on how you can improve or compensate in the areas you are less strong. This examination and early problem solving can be a valuable part of your feasibility study. Then you can translate your solutions into strengths in your business plan. This success-oriented approach to your business can turn what might have been a negative into a positive action plan that can favorably impress potential lenders or investors. An excellent resource for accomplishing this task is *The Rule Book of Business Plans for Startups* by Roger C. Rule.

Cronbaugh was just twenty-one years old when she went into business. Suddenly, she was in charge of hiring and directing people older and more experienced in the service industry than she. Looking back, she says, "There are times when I think about something I did or said and think, 'God, Tara, what were you thinking?' I just didn't know."

Even though Cronbaugh did two years of research on coffee and, while blindfolded, could probably name every blend of every brand ever made, she had not prepared herself for being in the service industry. "I should have worked at Starbucks for a year." Her salvation was her team.

Pick the Strongest Teams

You will always have naysayers. They'll include not only those you meet in the business community during your feasibility study, but those among friends and family members who believe they're simply looking out for you. These well meaning critics may want to protect you, but what you really need is positive reinforcement and, possibly, other forms of help from a team of people who believe in you. Almost all the women I talked with were clear about one thing: the support they received from family and friends was critical to their success. Most said that their families were never anything but positive. Debbi Fields did not have positive support from her parents, but she did from her husband.

Be picky. Choose your support team carefully because this group is very important. You will need reassurances and emotional backing when you hit stumbling blocks, including unanticipated success. Regardless of whether you need financial backing or someone to rely on to take up the slack, there are times you will need someone to be there for you. Sharon Leone had struggled in vain for a long time to land an account, then VISA called and placed an order for 62,500 chocolate coins. After the initial elation, she wondered, How am I going to accomplish this? Enter the support group, the team, the family.

For Mastroianni of Annie's Edibles, family was crucial to her success. One day, Mastroianni was working out with a trainer in Los Angeles; the next day, she was creating a menu for Academy Award winning actor Forest Whitaker. It happened that quickly. "Then, all the sudden I had seven clients, cooking three meals a day, seven days a week for each one. I needed my mom. Without my mom, I would have been struggling in the kitchen, crying."

Her mother quit her job as a magazine sales representative, moved to Santa Monica and began cooking with her daughter. "Nothing is better than your mom's cooking, right? Not only is she a great cook, she's a blessing." Mastroianni's father and step-mother were vital in creating brochures, sending them out to friends, and networking.

Without the proper network, all the money in the world would not account for a hill of beans. A company or idea can only be as good as the people working for it. One excellent player, alone, cannot send a team to the Super Bowl. Both a support team of friends and family and a reliable team of colleagues are crucial to your success. It is important to remember to treat them all with great respect.

Communicate Your Mission

The cohesion, effectiveness, and productivity of your teams are up to you. There are some rules that must be followed to build and maintain a successful team. As the leader, you must be fair, and you must be a team player at all times. You must share information with the team and think in a broader spectrum than when you were responsible only for yourself. You must consider first:

- What is good for the team?
- What is good for us?

Again, the U.S. women's bobsled team can be used as an example to illustrate a point. In 1994, the first ever U.S. women's bobsled team was created. Eight women were named and graced the pages of *Sports Illustrated.* It was a defining moment for women in sports. For the next three years, we struggled together as a team looking for funding, national and international support, and Olympic status. And in the those three years, many women came and went. The stress, we all understood, was too much for even the best of athletes. Still, there was a core of us who stood firm in our beliefs and athletic pursuits. We endured in-house fighting, paying our own way to competitions, holding raffles to raise money for equipment. We created bumper stickers ("I Brake for Bobsledders" and "Woman Driver and Proud of It"), sold merchandise, and begged for the U.S. women's bobsled program.

By the 1999 season, the U.S. women's team had national support, Olympic status, and major corporate funding. We worked hard to lay the ground work and pave the way for new athletes, which included establishing an excellent relationship with sledders overseas. During that season, however, a newcomer began to make claims of "founding the team." This left a sour taste in the mouths of the women who had fought so hard for the team. Instead of playing by the rules, this particular athlete was impatient to have immediate funding.

She did whatever it took to get what she wanted for herself, without any consideration for what was best for the rest of the women's bobsledding team. While she got what she wanted (first-rate equipment, first draw on team selection and races), initially, it changed how the entire team is viewed. Now, the international sledders don't share information or offer help as readily as before. As Stephenson warns, "The only thing you really own is your own integrity. However, you can give it away; but if you do, you are not likely to get it back." It was frustrating for those who'd been around during the tough times — the pioneers — to see the newcomer and nonteam-player get preferential treatment.

Then it was payback time. There almost always is and, for the ones who have broken the bonds of loyalty, it is usually unexpectedly painful. Once fractionalization begins, it's impossible to predict where it will end. To avoid its onset, armies never leave their wounded on the battlefield. The bond of comrades must not be broken. The athlete in question found she had no fellow athletes she could rely on at home or abroad.

This awful situation illustrates how formulating and holding to a mission statement is also important to your company or organization. What might seem like a good idea to one person might be detrimental to the company or to morale. Had we written down a clearly defined mission statement, this newer athlete would have better understood the rules of the game and had a better appreciation of acting for the good of the team. When a team's mission is clear, each member of the team can understand a group decision and be more inclined to honor it. In addition, when it is for the good of the team, a member can say *no* or override someone else's idea and still be a team player. A clear mission statement not only provides direction, it encourages team spirit.

There was never any question for the U.S. women's soccer team. They were a united front and understood from the beginning they were good enough to win the World Cup; also they realized they needed each other to do it. Because there were more than twenty women on the soccer team, you might think they would be more likely to fractionalize, but their mission was clearly defined for them. Team equates success.

When star player Joy Fawcett had her baby and saw how much stuff a baby needs, she realized she could not travel overseas with the team because they were limited to two suitcases. Fawcett says, when she surveyed what was needed [a portable crib, enormous supplies of diapers and formula, a stroller . . .], "I sat on the floor and cried. Who was I kidding? I would never be able to travel all over the world with all this stuff." Then came the team. One by one, each team member called to report she had one empty suitcase and would be able to handle one baby item.

Instead of celebrating the departure of a star athlete as an opportunity for someone else to step into her shoes, the team rallied for Fawcett, creating one of the most dynamic sports team in women's history. Scratch that: in history!

Be an Effective Leader

Ah, were being an effective leader as easy as the dictionary definition makes it seem: one who leads or guides. As the women in these pages learned, there is much more to effective leadership. Lynette Reed had to learn to delegate, counsel, and guide. Her greatest strength, she says, is not as a business person but as a people person.

An example of her leadership is illustrated by Illume, Inc.'s last holiday season. "We had over-committed ourselves," Reed says. "We were working seven days a week, double shifts. Our holiday season begins in August and we worked through until January. We had to hire on more temps, but didn't have the time to train them. Since our quality control is of the upmost importance, it put a lot of pressure on the supers. We can't let anything go out our doors that isn't right."

It was a lot of pressure for everyone. Never mind that they were all working double shifts or that it was scorching hot outside. And, never mind that the employees were all working in a nonair-conditioned warehouse with hot wax. The workers were getting tired, hot, and frustrated. But they didn't quit.

Instead of running a sweat shop, however, Reed is interested in keeping her employees. She offers constant pay raises and bonuses as incentives, and employees do stay on. In fact, Reed laughs, "We hire temps, but we always keep them. My husband is amazed people don't just quit, but I make sure people feel like they are part of the company."

For their holiday parties, Reed sends white stretch limousines to pick up the employees who don't own cars. A full-time masseuse is available year-round, so stressed out employees can get a chair massage anytime they need one. Reed had a cappuccino machine installed in the break room. And, during the hot months, she brings in free ice cream for everyone. "It is just a little thing to let them all know how appreciated they are. It's so easy to let them know."

With leadership abilities such as these, it is easy to see why Illume Candles, Inc. continues to grow at such incredible rates. From 1996 through 1998, Illume Candles, Inc. grew over 350 percent and netted more than $11 million in 1998.

Who would have thought this unemployed model could sell all her worldly possessions and end up the head of a multi-million dollar company only a few years later? But, she is quick to point out, were it not for her team, she would not be where she is today.

"I am not a business person, I am a people person," Reed says. "I am good at motivating people and keeping them together. I genuinely care about them, and my enthusiasm in the company rubs off on them."

Many of the business leaders I interviewed spoke of their businesses as though they were their babies. Reed is no exception; yet she learned early on that she needed to give up some control and delegate authority to other workers. "You have to give free range. Having someone stand over your shoulder all the time is no fun. But this was hard for me. You have to believe in the ability of others."

Ultimately, the most unpleasant tasks will come back to the CEO. Firing an employee is one of the most unpleasant responsibilities of Reed's position; but when complaints were coming in from female employees of sexual harassment, Reed had cause for alarm. Reed did not believe the harassment was intentional. It was, she says, just his way. But when the complaints continued after several warnings from management, her hands were tied. Reed had to do what was best for the team.

As Stephenson points out, effective leadership comes down to one thing: integrity. Knowing what is good for the team and for yourself will empower you.

Think Positively

You must also be able to deal with setbacks — both emotional and financial — as lessons learned. With each lesson you and your team learns, you can grow. Complaining and dropping your head as if to ask, Why me?, cannot fix your troubles or pick up team morale. Remember that everyone gets down once in a while. Learning not only how to pick your battles but what strategy to use in fighting back will determine much of your success.

In fact, when asked what mistakes Lynette Reed made and learned from, she refused to answer the question on those grounds. "I don't believe in mistakes. I look at everything as an experience." As long as you can recognize the stumbling blocks quickly enough, Reed says everything can be a valuable experience.

Rather than dive into a pit of despair, Fields of Mrs. Fields' Cookies accepted penalties levied against her new business, paid the $10,000 fine, and faced the extremely unpleasant task of firing her employees under the age of eighteen. As you might recall, state law prohibited these young people from using vital equipment in the cookie business. From that time on, Fields vowed to learn all the rules and penalties of the business world.

Jenai Lane and Cheryl Krueger-Horn learned even harder lessons. Each had an employee who embezzled money from their companies. In the case of Cheryl&Co., Krueger-Horn's employee managed to fund the renovation of his own home before she discovered the theft. Even worse, it was only because a friend of the employee turned him into the police that his theft was discovered. It could have easily been another six months before anyone realized what he was doing.

Lane lost several thousands of dollars before the thieving employee was caught. In the cases of both women, the employees were tried and convicted, serving the minimum amount of time. Neither Lane nor Krueger-Horn was able to recoup the money. It was lost. But both developed more structured checks and balance systems.

"Instead of one person doing everything," Lane says, "[now] one person does the deposits, another person handles billing. No one has access to wire transfers or money leaving the [corporate] account except me. I've talked to a lot of business owners who say theft is very common. It is unfortunate because it puts that added burden on the owner, but that's the way it is."

Create a Work Friendly Atmosphere

If you walk into the corporate headquarters of Jamba Juice in downtown San Francisco, California, you will likely walk right into the middle of a mean badminton game. Throughout the day, workers are allowed to break for a quick match to relieve stress and have a little fun. "With today's long hours on the job, there's a blurring in their lives between work and social activities," says Chris Baer, Jamba Juices' Vice-President of Human Resources. "Because we play here, too, employees think it's okay to spend the long hours here that they do."

Jamba Juice executives report a lower turnover rate and stress among employees. While some employers may take a dim view of this, Jamba Juice remains philosophical. Through a rousing game of badminton or any social activity, they believe their employees learn to better communicate with each other, thus building a stronger and healthier company.[4]

The point is, whether it's badminton at Jamba Juice or massages at Illume Candles, Inc. a friendly work atmosphere is a productive work atmosphere. Here are some other ideas and policies that have worked for businesswomen to ensure happy and stable workforces.

Allow Flex-Time

Allow for family to remain an important factor in your workers' lives. Many women in *Fortune* 500 and Wall Street firms have stated they limited family talk at work. In fact, many reported hiding the fact that they had children and, in some cases, that they were pregnant until it could no longer be kept a secret.

The reason: they feared they'd be discriminated against. There are those good ol' boys who still believe that women who are mothers are less reliable workers. While recent studies have shown just the opposite — out of necessity, mothers are more likely to hold the same position for longer periods than single men or women — too often women in business carry their family status like stigmas. By creating a family-friendly atmosphere, bosses find their employees are more productive, contribute more often, and behave more like teammates.

Get Everyone Involved

With Cheryl&Co., perhaps one of the most powerful days of the year is "Take a Child to Work Day" when employees spend a day with children from county orphanages. As Krueger-Horn tells it, when it comes time for the children to leave — the kids loaded down with all the cookies and treats they've chosen — there's not a dry eye in the company on either side. "We always hate to see them go. They are so sweet!"

What the company does for the community and the self-esteem of these individual children is evident, but what the children do for the workers at Cheryl&Co. is equally powerful. Perhaps more so.

Share the Credit

To be a team player, you must always share the credit with your team members, that is, your employees and partners. Give credit where it is due. Be sure to regularly acknowledge the efforts of others. Even if an idea does not pan out, you can give credit for positive thinking. Allowing subordinates to give input to company objectives enables them to feel invested and appreciated, and you inherit lots of good ideas.

When your employees feel part of the team or company, their productivity will reflect this. They will care about the mission. They will care about the product and the quality of packaging. It does not matter to Reed that the vast majority of her employees are very young and inexperienced. Because of the relaxed atmosphere at Illume Candles, the employees are motivated, eager to learn, and enthusiastic about their craft.

Each member of the employee team at Respect, Inc. chooses a charity of his or her choice and volunteers a full day every month. The employees may choose a different charity each month and are paid a full day's wages from the company for their time. But instead of looking at this as an expense to the company, Lane says, "Volunteering and giving to non-profit organizations is a selfish thing, as well, because it makes *you* feel good. People have forgotten that. You get something very real and valuable and tangible that stays with you at the end of the day."

Be a Good Listener

This is an area where women both excel and get into trouble. We listen well, but we often confuse listening and communicating with close relationships. Good communication with your team does not mean you have to be everybody's buddy. Openness, honesty, and fairness are what determine good communication. By establishing yourself as a good listener and a fair manager, you will earn the respect of your team members. In order to lead effectively, you must temper your willingness to share and bond with a little distance. Maintain a bit of mystery with your employees. As they say in show business, always leave them wanting more.

An important part of communicating is trusting, being able to rely on one another. Reed says, "In addition to being a good listener, it is important to know how to delegate. No one will do things the way you would do it, and that's okay! You have to learn to trust your team and appreciate the way they approach things." Don't ever forget that you are all in this together. It may be your business, but you can't succeed — and probably wouldn't want to try — without your team.

Chapter 8

Casualties of Success

—

B ecause women have always excelled in the art of communication, it's no surprise that women executives are efficient and
excellent leaders or that communication and positive reinforcement are perceived as their greatest leadership qualities. Yet, it's
difficult to find a time in history when personal relationships were in
more turmoil.

"Women have a harder time now, more than ever before," Lynette
Reed says. It is the typical Supermom complex she is describing. "Our
moms knew what they were supposed to do." While Reed agrees women
fare better now in terms of progress, education, and acceptance, the burden of doing it all has been added.

There was a defining moment for Reed, she says, as she held her two-
year-old son, Harris, on her left hip and reached into the dryer to pull out
a load of clothes while talking business on her telephone head-set — all
while she kept a careful eye on the clock because dinner was in the oven.

"I was so mad at my husband. I felt like everything was my responsibility. I had over seventy employees, was running my own business, my
house, and watching Harris. All without an assistant. Could any man
have done that?" Not very many try.

"As women, we are supposed to do it all, but if we need help, we feel
like failures." That, in fact, is one of the reasons some experts believe

women procrastinate. We push everything to the edge at all times because we are trying to give service to every detail of every different aspect in our lives at every given moment. If someone else cooks meals for our family or cleans our house, we have failed. If we need to call for assistance in our work, we have let our management abilities slip.

Even supermodel Kathy Ireland uses a head-set telephone, so she can conduct business over the phone and do house chores at the same time. When professional basketball player Valerie Still was going into an American Basketball League play-off, she found herself wondering if her husband brought the baby's diaper bag.

Roles of a Modern Woman

What can we do about it? Experts suggest is that we learn from our male counterparts and adopt some of the expediting skills they have used for centuries. Expect assistance from the team to make the game plan run more smoothly. It is something Reed finally accepted. "I'm not doing [everything] anymore," she laughed. "Life has been so much easier."

Reed had to be booked into the hospital for overnight observation when she developed strange heart palpitations and chest pains.

Lynette Reed and Harris in the warehouse

"Turns out it was stress," but it was enough to turn her around. Now she has someone who comes in to clean the house, and she accepts help more willingly.

Still, the responsibility of the family lands squarely on the shoulders of the woman in most households, even if she is a businesswoman. In fact, my initial interview with Reed was rescheduled several days in a row because of a sick child. Harris had a temperature of almost 105 degrees, keeping Reed home from the office for the entire week.

Tara Cronbaugh was introduced to how hectic life would become as a businesswoman and mother when she received a fax from a national coffee trade show. Cronbaugh had earned a reputation as key speaker, so it was not unusual for her to receive an urgent fax asking her to talk to a business group that day. As Cronbaugh was leaving her apartment at 6:00 A.M., she dashed a fax back to the trade show: "Can't. I'm in labor!"

I talked a lot about children with most of the women I interviewed. After all, for many women, the kids play such a vital role in how the day can go, what hours can be kept, what work can be accomplished, and how much guilt we feel. How could we not talk about them?

Tara Cronbaugh, McKenna, and friend

Job sharing was another hot topic. As part of the Supermom phenomenon, Reed and several others talked about the everyday chores of running a household that fall directly on a woman's shoulders. It was reaffirmed to me many times by successful businesswomen: in order to make a business work, you must give it 100 percent. That means something in your personal life must give way. This can become quite a juggling act when the quality of other peoples' lives depend on the woman in question. On more than one occasion, an overextended woman asked, "Why does all the responsibility land in my lap?"

This is a tricky issue. For some, this is the way of the world. It has always been this way, and it always will. For others, this is nonsense. During my work on *Entering the Mother Zone*, I found similar complaints from new mothers. Exhausted from nursing and caring for the new baby, many resented the lack of participation from their husbands. Dr. Rick Petosa of Ohio State University who studies the effects of nursing on new mothers and their families says this doesn't have to be. Job sharing among active couples becomes critical for the happiness of both mom and dad. "Enlightened couples can and do job share, he says, making personal adjustments along the way."

All the women I interviewed regarded family support as paramount to success. Many, such as Fields and Craig, said without the support of their husbands, their businesses simply would not exist today. Parents and siblings were particularly important for Mastroianni, Jacobs, Krueger-Horn, and Wolan. Both Mastroianni's and Jacobs' mothers moved to Los Angeles to help their daughters' businesses. Krueger-Horn's brother moved to Columbus to help her start the business. My own parents were instrumental in each and every one of my ventures. But for women whose family members — specifically their significant others — were less than supportive, or even jealous of their successes, the strain on the relationships was destructive.

Craig nailed it on the head when asked what advice she could give up-and-coming entrepreneurs. She said, "You have to ask yourself, 'What is it I will have to give up to make the business successful?' Is it family time, staying at home, taking trips? Whatever it is, you must weigh how important the business is to you, particularly today. Because the market is so competitive, it requires total focus on your part. Like the old saying goes, 'If you can't stand the heat, stay out of the kitchen,' or in this case, the business world.

"Motherhood is a lot harder," says Jennifer Maxwell, "because you worry about everything. You want to do everything perfectly, but there just isn't enough time in the day. I realize that world doesn't exist. They [children] are the source of my joy. They are not a burden and not work." But, oh, how it can seem that way.

Also, Maxwell reminds us, guilt is a huge part of motherhood. "Women get wrapped up in the guilt. Being everywhere and doing everything for their kids, and the guilt can grow. It has a domino effect that touches everything."

Maxwell's observations resonated with what other women said about the strain a business can put on relationships. For those who have children, ignoring parenting responsibilities is not an option. But, all too often, relationship responsibilities for a husband, boyfriend, or significant other are deprioritized for the sake of the business. Because her husband was such an integral part of her success, Craig is an exception; but the majority of businesswomen share other experiences.

When calling Valerie Coolidge of Gourmet Gifts after six months had elapsed, I found a lot had changed for her and her company. "Family became the major issue," Coolidge said. "I had started a business with a faulty conception. I wanted to base a business from home so I could be all things. I could take care of my children, my home, and have a business at the same time. But it didn't take any time at all for this thing to get out of control. It was a zoo. A nightmare. My husband was ready to jump ship. I had seven employees working in the house, peanuts everywhere. The house was a mess. It was too much for all of us."

In fact, Coolidge's mentor, Krueger-Horn, served as an example in more ways than one. Coolidge says she saw the devastation in Krueger-Horn's personal life caused by her business. "I made the decision I didn't want that to happen to me," Coolidge says. "I saw the stakes that she [Krueger-Horn] put forward and I didn't want that. I was thankful I saw it. I wanted my family. I wanted my husband."

So, having made up her mind, Coolidge placed an ad in the business section of the newspaper. "I decided I would have to find a buyer. In the first week I got a buyer at full price and closed without a hitch. It was meant to be. It all happened too perfectly, and my life has been so much better."

Coolidge quickly made her exit from the world Tess Rano was just stepping into. As the highly energetic kick-boxing martial arts instructor prepared to start her own karate school, she found her husband to be less than supportive.

Tess Rano teaching a kickboxing class

"He's always been so supportive of everyone around him. He is very positive and encouraging to other people, so I had to ask him why was he being so negative with me?" He was questioning his wife's business skills and background and wondering out loud why she was taking on this risky venture.

I reminded her that most women agreed: their significant others weren't really questioning their abilities but were suddenly wondering how and where they fit into what's going on. "That's it exactly," Rano confirmed. The prospect of a new business poses an immediate threat to the family: how do we figure in?

Jenai Lane of Respect, Inc. supposes, "As women become more successful in our society, the men are more threatened." The men, she points out, are not entirely to blame. "Our culture teaches men they should be the bread winners, and a woman's profession comes second."

But her business was where her passion lay. As Lane recalls, she could have worked day and night, she was so excited about her new life. Krueger-Horn felt the same way. However, as they became more successful in their businesses, things began to unravel at home.

While working on other books about national, professional, and Olympic athletes, I spoke with women such as Mary Lou Retton, Cory Everson, Sheryl Swoopes, Valerie Still. All of them pointed out the reality that expectations of male athletes are completely different from the demands placed on female athletes. As Swoopes proposed, "Do you think Michael Jordan has to worry about diaper bags, changes of clothes, and bottles going into a game?"

The role that male athletes play in the public sector is just that: athlete. As role models they have an awesome vertical leap, amazing hang time, outstanding times in the forty-yard dash. They can jump, catch, throw, and hit like nobody's business.

But for female athletes, being a mother is also very much a part of who they are. Motherhood is considered in contracts and is mentioned over and over again in the press. Fortunately, female athletes believe parenthood is a good thing — something to be proud of — and wonder why the same is not true for men. Perhaps if more male athletes were also known as good, responsible, loving fathers, there would be a different perception of the importance among young boys and men of a father's role in society.

I remember when I was headed to the first International World Cup for women bobsledders in Alberta, Canada, and a major player in the sports world asked me, "Are you a mother or an athlete?" You see, in the eyes of many, you can't be both. One, it is believed, will have to give way to the other — as if a person can only be one thing, fill one role.

Sadly, the business world is no different. Krueger-Horn, twice divorced, says there is no question as to why the marriages failed. Her work requires long, hard days. It demanded much of her attention and that is, she says, something that most men are not equipped to handle. Coolidge sold her business to save her marriage. These pressures have been felt by many.

Also, many women reported the conscious or unconscious attempts by their significant others to sabotage their efforts in the business world. As Valerie Still was preparing herself to go into the American Basketball League's playoffs — where she made sports history — her husband complained that the house was a disaster and there had been too few home-cooked meals.

Still is not alone. Most women have witnessed or experienced businesses or projects becoming threats to significant others. Whatever takes a woman's attention away from her family becomes the thing that is the most threatening. "It comes down to where you are putting your energy," says Lane. "Where does your real passion lie?" Although Western countries are the most progressive cultures in terms of women's rights, most boys are still raised with the notion and first-hand experience that women are the caregivers — to the entire family unit.

"It's tough work juggling motherhood and business," Cronbaugh affirms. "It's tough because I make it that way. I thrive off of my work, and I love going to work. I used to love my sleep, too," she laughs. "Now, I don't care. I thrive off of the craziness of work. You get used to it, then things get a little easier. At first, I thought, 'How can I do this?' Now, if I sit down to watch Oprah, I feel guilty. I've had to learn how to juggle things to make them work."

Redefine Your Roles

Again, it all comes down to taking risks. Part of being a risk-taker is breaking away from your comfort zones. This is another reason why so many experts stress the importance of picking a strong, positive team.

They will be the people who help you through the stormy weather; and there will be stormy weather.

Whenever women brake with conformity and begin taking risks, they must run the gauntlet which includes facing harsh criticism, often from other women. If you remember Marcia Clark, the attorney who was the prosecutor in the O.J. Simpson trial, you probably also remember the reports of how she was neglecting her own children by working such long hours. Haven't male attorneys been doing the same thing for centuries with nary a whisper or comment?

What was most disturbing was that some of her most vocal critics were other women. While interviewing professional women basketball players, I was amazed by how many former Olympic teammates and players in the WNBA protested when Sheryl Swoopes became pregnant just after she signed a contract with the Houston Comets. The discriminatory myth that women in sports would only stick with a program until they can get married and pregnant persisted and haunted even those who chose to remain single or childless.

Finally, the trial-that-never-seemed-to-end ended for Clark. Swoopes gave birth to a healthy boy and came back as strong as ever, quieting her critics and challenging the myth. Just as the lawyer and the athlete, as a businesswoman you must prove yourself again and again both as a professional and a family member. Here, the skills of a true leader must come into play. Job sharing is important as are the abilities to think fast on your feet, make adjustments, and work out compromises.

There must be, Lane says, a balance. "It comes down to where you are putting your energy. Where does your passion lie?" More precisely, you must determine how to make things work more efficiently. For some it may be a matter of job sharing and compromise. For others, it may mean reprioritizing your business and personal affairs. Again, as Craig says, you have to decide what your priorities are and proceed from there. Can you run a businesses with only a fifty percent interest? Can you run a marriage or relationship that way?

For years women in business have been successfully modifying the rules of the game in their businesses and personal relationships to make both work more efficiently and effectively. As I spoke with Reed over the telephone I could hear people piling into her house. Because her business has expanded so rapidly, she likes to hold company meetings in her dining room. "I live just five minutes away so I can work from home." And, she adds, her dining room is a much more creative environment for her and her employees.

One of the beauties of starting their own companies for many women is that they have been able to use their homes as headquarters. Krueger-Horn, Blackmon, and Leone all started that way. By creating their own flex time hours for their families and businesses, they are able, as some have expressed, "to have it all." In recent years, however, there have been articles and features about this subject. Should we be trying to do it all? Is it good for us? Is it good for our children? There is a lot of guilt associated with this whole topic of Supermom.

While writing *Entering the MotherZone*, I had the opportunity to ask mother-athletes such as Mary Lou Retton, Gwen Torrence, Peggy Fleming, and Sheryl Swoopes if they believed being professional athletes made them better mothers. None of them hesitated with their answers. No question. Because they are busy, healthy, and living out their dreams, they all believe they are sending very positive messages to their children. They are teaching them to be happy, healthy, and self-reliant. They are teaching them that, with hard work, dreams can come true.

The businesswomen I talked with are no exception. For all the highs and lows the business world brought them, for all the long hours and anxious times of waiting for shipments to arrive or openings to go as scheduled, the benefits for these women have been undeniable. For each one, self-esteem sky-rocketed as she began to see her dreams, hopes, and hard work come to fruition.

Case in point. Lynette Reed opted out of college for a career in modeling and acting.

Some of Lynette Reed's elegant candles

The lack of a degree wasn't an issue for years until she entered the world of business and high finance. Suddenly, she felt like she was free-falling. Too many times she was told that because she didn't have a college background she would never make it. Financial lenders, bankers, and even friends had warned Reed not to go into business. They believed that it was something she could never pull off. After all, what experience or education did she have?

"Everyone is insecure about something. For me, it's college." A real highlight in Reed's career came in the fall of 1998 when she received a phone call from UCLA's Anderson School of Business. "They wanted to use Illume as a case study."

While a group of twelve MBA students analyzed Reed's business approach and the business itself, Reed sneaked into the back of the class. She quietly settled herself into a chair and watched and listened. It was quite a moment for Reed as she heard these MBAs discuss how she was successfully operating her own business.

"I got to sit in on a class. It was my first college class. I felt so validated."

Chapter 9

Making It Work

—

Not one of the women in this book, no matter how successful she is today, will tell you that her voyage into the world of business was all smooth sailing. Earning the designation magnate is like earning an academic degree — there are a lot of all-nighters, a lot of missed deadlines, and a lot of poor marks in various subjects. But every failure is seen as a lesson learned, every setback used to take another step forward. As each women pressed forward on her journey to success, she figured out what worked for her.

To become a magnate, each woman mastered two importance characteristics, identified by Ed Moldt as key qualities for a successful entrepreneur: to be able to modify her behavior and to think fast on her feet.

When Success Comes Fast

Shortly after Lynette Reed opened her candle store, against the protests of friends and family, Melanie Griffith wandered in during the Christmas season and purchased 120 gift baskets. Essentially, that was the greatest gift Reed had ever received because Hollywood executives and celebrities quickly found out about the chic candle shop. Today, Illume Candles, Inc. publishes a fun newsletter, naming some of its celebrity patrons, such as Demi Moore, Courtney Love, Barbra Streisand, Anthony Edwards, Laurence Fishburne, Alanis Morisette, Kristen Johnson, James Cameron, and Sandra Bullock. *Vanity Fair, In-Style, Working*

Woman, House Beautiful, Bon Appetit, Self, Mode, and *W,* to name a few, have featured the growing company in their magazines. All because an immensely popular actress walked into Reed's store and liked what she saw. You can bet Reed is a big Melanie Griffith fan.

Reed was very lucky. She had done little to no research, but gut instinct told her that opening a shop in that particular location would give her the best business. She was right. Then "I thought, 'Well, gee, if things went this well at this store, I should open another." So Reed opened a store in Santa Monica, and six months later she decided to close the door. Reed took it in stride. "I tried. It didn't work out," she says, "but it was okay because I had the other store, so I just moved the stock over [to the first store]." As soon as she realized retail expansion was not going to be as successful as she hoped, she got out quickly. Just as Moldt suggests, always leave room for flexibility.

"I did lose a lot of money. Not what would be considered a lot of money by some in the business world, but it was a lot for me." However, that wasn't Reed's first miscalculation. "We lost a lot on our first catalogue, too. We went all gung-ho without doing any research. We didn't really understand what we were doing."

It is this impulsive nature that got Reed into trouble and that Moldt warns about. Yet, it is also this risk-taking attitude that got her candle shop started in the first place. She was able to stay afloat because of her ability to modify her behavior and think fast on her feet.

Throughout her first three years in business, Reed did not make her own candles; she purchased them from other manufacturers. She liked candles and had an eye for what consumers liked.

"Then one of my manufacturers didn't want to make candles anymore, so I bought the equipment from her, and she taught me how to make candles. She just taught me the basic designs, then I taught myself how to use colors and scents. I've always liked working with my hands. That is my talent. That's the easy part. Once I got my hands in the wax, I felt really confident about what I was doing."

A hidden benefit was the way she approached the business world, Reed says. As a vendor for many manufacturers, she learned what customers wanted and liked. "Because I was with customers day in and day out, I knew what their tastes were, and I could see the mistakes the manufacturers were making." She used that consumer knowledge to become more sophisticated in her candle making by designing an extensive line of colored and scented candles.

"Then I started going to the big trade shows. The bigger companies would stop by, place sample orders to see if they liked the candles." They did. Reed attracted the attention of the some of the largest department and catalogue stores in the country. Instead of mass producing their special candles under Illume's name, Reed put private labels on the candles for the bigger stores.

Smaller boutiques continued to carry the exclusive Illume Candle brand. "I just know my customers. The smaller stores would be upset if they saw us in Macy's or Nordstrom's." For someone who was intimidated about setting foot on a college campus, that was a pretty savvy business move.

"I learn quickly," Reed laughs.

Day to Day Operations

Jenai Lane designed jewelry in her spare time in college, but she had no means to manufacture the creations of her passion until a car accident settlement gave her $3,000. She began selling her jewelry in small boutiques on consignment. But she wasn't satisfied. She needed to land bigger accounts if she ever expected to expand, and she wanted to expand. But how? How could she break into the jewelry manufacturing business. Then, one day, the answer came to her.

"I was sitting in a café when I saw this woman walking down the street, pushing this huge display rack." It was full of all kinds of jewelry similar to the kind Lane designed. "I stopped her and asked her where she was going with all the jewelry. She said, 'Well, I'm a jewelry sales rep.' I just smiled and said, 'Well, I'm looking for someone to help me.' Just like that."

But even as Lane began to land large accounts, she could not get any financial institutions to take her seriously. In fact, she had gotten an account with Macy's Department store but was still unable to get the funding to fill the orders. This was a surprise. With a name like Macy's banging at your door, it was hard to imagine any bank would turn Lane away. "They literally laughed me out the door. I wasn't asking for that much — $10,000. I had impeccable credit. I couldn't understand it.

"But I had no business experience. Banking institutions are so sexist. You're starting to see a change, but the money they lend to women is still not comparable to [that for] men."

Moldt suggests that it is unnecessary to take a large financial risk, such as putting a second mortgage on a house to fund your business. If you look hard enough, he says, you will find a program that can help you.

That is precisely what Lane did, finding a local women's organization in her San Francisco neighborhood that could help her — the Women's Initiative for Self-Employment (WISE). "They have these courses for low-income women. Once you complete the course, you are eligible for $2,000, then $10,000, then $20,000. It is cyclical, so you can put money directly into your sales and pay the loan back. It was only after I paid back a $20,000 loan that the banks started to take me seriously."

"The key to success," says Lane, "is being willing to take risks. The trouble is if you don't risk anything, you risk even more. That is how I perceive the world. It is like not living your dream. You have to take the risks to get the rewards." The rewards: Lane's company was named one of the fifty fastest growing companies in the United States, and Lane was named Woman Entrepreneur of the Year for 1998.

Steps to Success

Women get into business for a variety of reasons. Passion, we believe, is a prerequisite for success. Jenny Craig's passion was born out of fear — fear she might die at an early age like her mother and might not see her children grow or enjoy her future grandchildren. Craig was determined that would not happen and set out to change her life.

Once true passion took hold, the world around her began to change. What Craig has done for herself, the diet and food industries, and millions of people around the world is the strongest testament there is to passion's role in the business world.

Craig took all the recommended steps for developing a successful business while creating the multi-billion dollar corporation she owns. She:

• Set her goal
• Understood her market
• Researched several aspects of the business and her products
• Identified her resources
• Identified and adapted to the best location
• Learned what she needed to know
• Developed her marketing skills
• Honed her people skills
• Believed in herself and her goal

At age fifty, Craig and her husband, Sid, packed all their belongings, said good-bye to the family, and headed off to Australia to start up their own business. A new home in a new culture and, essentially, a new world would be a terrifying prospect for many people, but to Craig it was the adventure of a lifetime.

She and her husband were going for broke. They had a great concept. They had the experience, the passion, and the drive. Now, they were off for the biggest test of their lives. But it was not an overnight success story.

"You have to understand, I've been doing this since 1958. That was a time when no one talked about diets or cholesterol or how food effects our overall health." But Craig made it her mission to find out everything she could.

Jenny Craig learned about healthy living

Craig is literally a self-taught entrepreneur. She joined a gym to get back into shape and lose the more than forty-five pounds she gained during a pregnancy. She was very serious about her weight loss, and she began to learn more and more about the importance of healthy living. So impressed were the owners of the gym she frequented, they offered her a job. She worked as an instructor, then as manager. This, she says, was the beginning of her career. While she did not yet know what she was in for, she knew she had found her niche. This was her calling.

Having outgrown the managerial role, Craig wanted more from the business world, so she invested in her own gym. "Business is a lot like lifting weights," Craig says. "You don't join a gym and begin lifting 100 pounds. You have to work up to it, first lifting twenty pounds, then more and more."

Enter Sid Craig. Sid, owner of the California-based fitness salon Body Contour, met his future wife when he established a Body Contours in New Orleans. Jenny Craig came on board wanting to learn more about the business. It was not long before she was the company's National Director of Operations. In 1979, the Craigs married and three years later sold their business to move to Australia to begin anew.

Why Australia?

In the 1980s, the weight management market was already pretty competitive, and the Craigs were looking for an untapped market. "There was no comprehensive weight loss program on the market in Australia; and it was ideal for us because it was an English-speaking country which was, obviously, very important to us."

Even before the move, however, the Craigs had a strategic plan: marketing, marketing, marketing. Before the first Jenny Craig Center door was ever opened, the Craigs launched a heavy commercial campaign, and Jenny Craig appeared on the "Bert Newton Show" — the Australian equivalent of the "Johnny Carson Show."

The Craigs' marketing strategy is reminiscent of the old 1962 Doris Day and Rock Hudson movie, *Lover Come Back*. In the movie, Hudson invents an imaginary product so his advertising company can experiment with a saturation campaign. Before it was ever out, people lined up and waited to buy the non-existent product.

The saturation campaign worked. Australians were chomping at the bit in the same way, wanting to learn more about Jenny Craig before the centers were even open for business. When she appeared on his show, Newton asked over and over when they would open. "I could only say, 'Soon, soon.' The show aired on Sunday nights, so over the weekend we let him know we would open on Monday. That Monday morning, there were so many people we literally had to take numbers." Talk about knowing your market.

Understanding your consumers and how to market to them is key to success. Whereas companies like Illume Candles, Inc. or Mrs. Fields' Cookies could grow by word of mouth, the Craigs understood that their business would succeed or fail depending on how quickly they engaged the market. They went for complete saturation, opening nine stores at once. Within one year, they opened a total of fifty stores — a record in Australia that remains unbroken.

Obviously, the Craigs' first budget priority was for advertising. The second item on their list was food. When they arrived in Australia, they contracted with the best nutritionists and top doctors in behavior modification, all of whom are still on board today. However, they quickly ran into a problem with vendors. The Craigs, like Cozy Wolan, learned food manufacturers wouldn't produce small orders. "We had to convince them that we would be expanding. We had to make them believe that we would be saturating the country."

That was where their marketing techniques came into play. Because of the many commercials and their big hit on the "Bert Newton Show," the food manufacturer had indeed heard of them. Supplying the Craigs was a risk they were willing to take.

"We became their biggest account," Jenny says.

Their marketing scheme was brilliantly played. But most experts would agree that the Craigs are an exception. Because they were already established financially, they did not have to take the same kinds of risks as most of the women in this book. Then again, they were willing to take some remarkable chances by leaving their home and shedding the idea of boundaries to make the business work. It was less a matter of money, for the Craigs, than of redefining boundaries.

Boundary Issues

A boundary issue was key for the Craigs. However, the primary issues for most women are money and business know-how. You have a fantastic idea, but you have no idea how to market it. These are the reasons Joy Mangano sat on and lost her first invention and the reasons most ideas and dreams go unfulfilled. But technology is changing all that. Private businesses are now popping up faster than ever before.

Who would have thought someone could sell tumbleweeds and actually turn a profit. Now, Linda Katz and the Prairie Tumbleweed Farm's Internet home page receive some 400 hits a day. "There are no taxes over the Internet and access to the market is free. I would have had to go out and buy advertisement space in the papers, but this is free!" Katz laughs. Who would have thought?

Now, Katz spends much of her day responding to mail, filling orders, and answering questions. "The other day, someone contacted us, wanting to buy tumbleweed seeds," she laughs. "Tumbleweed seeds! Sometimes we just sit back and laugh about this whole thing. We can't believe how it's taken off. I knew the Internet was fast, but I had no idea at the time that we would get this kind of response." It is the perfect marketing tool for a growing business.

Mangano also took advantage of modern technology. Retailer after retailer turned Mangano and her Miracle Mop away. As she says, they just didn't understand. "Men don't mop!" She knew she had something women would want, however, marketing was a problem. It's hard to sell something that no one sees. Enter QVC's home-shopping network.

"I live in a time and place in history that I could do this," she says. Mangano called the production department at QVC and requested their guidelines for submitting a product. "I can go on QVC in front of sixty million people all the time. QVC loves to showcase new ideas!" And showcase they did. The Miracle Mop was a huge success, allowing Mangano to step into the role of full-time inventor. In the past year, Mangano has showcased over half a dozen other ideas on QVC and is now selling items like the RollyKit (a jewelry box that rolls into a neat, small round package for traveling) in retail stores around the country.

"Everyone has an idea. The question is," she wonders, "what are you going to do with it?"

Lessons Learned the Hard Way

Rather than a product, Tara Cronbaugh had a concept to sell. Unlike the Craigs, however, she was unwilling to wait fifteen years to research her dream. As soon as her feasibility study showed promise, Cronbaugh was off and running.

Her only experience in the business world was working at her uncle's truck washing business when she was in high school. Since her uncle wasn't much into dealing with billing and other paperwork, Cronbaugh took care of that aspect of his business.

But it wasn't until she visited her brother at the University of California in Berkeley that Cronbaugh experienced the first brush with her calling. A trendy coffee shop that served espresso to college students had Cronbaugh wishing there was such a place in her hometown of Iowa City. "It was just a cool place to hang out," she says. In the eyes of a twenty-year-old, what could be more exciting?

Unlike most twenty-year-olds, however, Cronbaugh didn't forget about it when she returned to the University of Iowa. It nagged at her. What if . . . ? She began talking to everyone about it. Her friends, family, and sorority sisters.

"I can tell you that I have one distinct memory that jumps out at me. This was during my sorority days. I was sitting on the floor talking about this idea. We were talking about how neat it would be to do this and that . . . one of my sisters was really into the conversation." It was all the encouragement Cronbaugh needed. "All of a sudden the conversation really clicked, and I knew I wanted it. I wanted the coffee house. I knew, also, I needed a business plan, but what is a business plan? I didn't even know. That's why I took the [entrepreneurs] class. I had to see if it was for me."

As you know, it was. Cronbaugh's challenge was not about boundaries or redefining who she was, hers was to learn what she wanted to know and to scrape together start-up money. With the support of her network, which included the University of Iowa's business staff, Cronbaugh had more security than she realized when she made her decision. Her passion triumphed over her doubts and, despite her age and lack of experience, she went for it.

She went to the Small Business Development Center (SBDC) on campus where she learned even more about formatting her business plan, networking, and how to approach banks. "They were a great resource for me," she says. Once Cronbaugh had her business plan, the SBDC suggested she go to her state's Targeted Small Business program where she was given a grant. With the grant, she was able to go to the banks and get a loan for the rest of the capital she needed.

Although, upon reflection, she thinks she should have worked at Starbucks for a year to gain some experience before opening her first establishment in the book store, Tara became the owner of four successful coffee establishments. In an average day, the four locations serve more than 2,000 customers.

During the first few years, Cronbaugh ordered supplies, dealt with vendors and leasing agents, prepared quarterly tax reports, tracked inventory, and was the public relations manager. In addition, Cronbaugh created the training and coffee blends manuals all potential employees must study, then pass a two-hour exam. Like Fields, Cronbaugh set a standard of quality that has earned her a reputation of excellence.

Cronbaugh and McKenna sharing a cookie in an Iowa City Coffee Company establishment

Like everyone else, Cronbaugh has had her fair share of bad times. In her first year, the turnover rate of employees was very high. "My first year, I had 120 W-2s. I didn't know what I was doing. I really didn't know how to handle employees. It was all so new to me. Now we don't even have a firing policy. It sounds funny, but no one gets fired here. Everyone is so happy."

Cronbaugh still faces growing pains. The day I spoke with her, she was stressed over the delayed grand opening of her fourth store. "Our landlord still has work that has to be done, our general contractor has more work, and the drywall keeps cracking," she laughs. "But we like the headaches."

Lisa Nistico thought she knew everything she needed to know before stepping into the world of business. In fact, she had a pretty nice set up because she purchased Gourmet Gifts from Valerie Coolidge. It already had an established clientele, so Nistico couldn't lose.

"I was looking for something I could do from home. Cooking had always been a hobby of mine and my mother was a professional cook, so this seemed perfect," Nistico says. "I asked Valerie about all the negatives. She told me that she'd wanted a part-time business, but this had turned into a full-time deal. I was prepared for that." What she was not prepared for, however, was botched batches of chocolate.

Nistico purchased Gourmet Gifts on September 1, 1998, at the beginning of the holiday rush. "Right away I was extremely busy. Even though Valerie told me everything, it took me a while to adjust." Her first few weeks in the business world were a nightmare. "At least sixty percent of all the chocolate would crack or would not sit up properly on the spoon. Chocolate is so finicky. I was having to redo over sixty per cent of my work," she says. That was when the big order came. In the middle of her crisis, Cheryl&Co. called wanting 7,000 spoons.

"It was a lot of trial by error. More error than anything," she laughs, "but I figured it out. Every room is different. Even the humidity is different in each room. I had to add more fans to have the chocolate cool down more quickly, but it all worked out." She learned to think fast on her feet and modify her behavior: characteristics which have proven essential for establishing a business and for guiding it as it grows.

Busy cookie bakers in the ultra clean kitchens of Cheryl&Co.

Cozy Wolan had no water on opening day. Krueger-Horn opened a week late after hundreds of batches of flat cookies. Lynette Reed had no money left over to stock her store after putting all her money into the mandatory three months rent — there was an echo in her store for the grand opening. Everyone has horror stories.

Gretchen Leddy learned the hard way that before she hired a cake decorator she should see the person's work. "I hired one woman because I took her at her word. However, when I saw what she could do, I realized I could have done the same thing. Now, as part of the hiring process, I give the applicant an hour to make and decorate a cake." Since then, hiring is based on actual quality of work, not what is printed on a résumé.

Fields did not realize that writing down the ingredients to Mrs. Fields' famous cookies could someday avert a crisis.

Lane didn't realize the importance of a nondisclosure form and had her ideas stolen by what she thought was a highly reputable company. Later, she found out a sales rep was billing her for mileage and turning in receipts for false purchases.

Reed discovered that the business world operated on a different time table than the banks. "My customers were supposed to pay in thirty days, but no one pays in thirty days. I know that now. It's more like forty-five days. But I was expected to pay in thirty days. I had no leeway. I was getting really big orders but wasn't able to fill them because I did not have the money."

Just as Krueger-Horn and Lane learned to establish a checks and balance system to protect their companies against embezzlement, Reed had to learn a new bookkeeping system that would overlap receivables and orders and provide a revolving system for credit.

Crucial to Annalisa Mastroianni's growth was learning the value of writing down ingredients and menus and the importance of billing accounts receivable. She had no grand plan for going into business. She was just minding her own business, working out with a trainer, when he approached her with the idea of catering special diets for his exclusive clientele. Mastroianni was an excellent cook and had a background in the restaurant business, but once the business took off — and take off it did — she learned some valuable lessons the hard way.

"Looking back, I realize I should have invested more money into my business. It would have grown more quickly, but I was afraid of going into debt. I should have been more active in sales, but I wasn't a salesperson. I never cared about that kind of thing. But the biggest thing I learned," she laughs, "was billing." Mastroianni had been paying for her inventory on her credit cards, which was a problem because her celebrity clients were not always prompt with their payments. "I learned to start billing for the week up front."

The biggest threat to her fledgling company, Annie's Edibles, came when Mastroianni was stricken with kidney stones. "One minute I'm walking around shopping, two hours later I'm in the hospital, in the emergency room. Just as Fields' investors had warned her, Mastroianni suddenly found herself facing the fact that nothing was written down. "I have a gift where I can keep everything in my head. But I learned my lesson. I hadn't planned on being down. I thought I was going to drop dead from the pain. Whoever plans for kidney stones? I didn't even have a delivery list written out. I had done everything myself. I knew where I was going. Stupid. Stupid."

Lying in the hospital, Mastroianni had to talk her fiancé and a kitchen helper through the menu plans and delivery routes. Since then, she has created menu and delivery books.

Most problems can be overcome if you are flexible and creative. Mastroianni, like the others, learned to think fast and modify her behavior. As these women have demonstrated, you must challenge your boundaries. Whether they are physical location, family, friends, or work obligations, there are undoubtedly ways you can work around the system and make your dreams come true, too. There are countless organizations you can call for help, but the initial step is yours.

You must pick up the phone.

You must feel deeply enough about your vision (what you want to accomplish) and your worthiness to achieve success to do what is necessary to accomplish it. When you can feel your dream, feel the passion, you will have the foundation necessary to generate sufficient energy, inspiration, and creativity, to make it come true — albeit with modifications and enhancements along the way.

The foundation for success of rising stars Yee and Slater is passion. "It's amazing that you can talk about something and people will believe it. I mean, we made up the name Massage Away over a Chinese dinner," laughs Slater, who still remembers their first paying customer with great amusement. "He said, 'So, who do I make this check out to?' and I remember thinking: Oh, my God, he doesn't know this isn't real. But it was. It is. It is just a tremendous thing when you take the dreams out of your head and put them to paper. You have to start believing in yourself to make things happen."

Remember: passion rules.

Chapter 10

Building a Network

A common thread among successful businesswomen is the burning desire for a more significant involvement in their world than could be achieved by working for someone else. By redefining their boundaries and taking risks, they have been able to make their dreams come true. Passion *can* move mountains. However, before you can move that proverbial mountain, you must learn how to network. Understanding then acting upon your passion and networking are two extremely important aspects of building a business. Too often, they are neglected steps.

You may not know yet what you want to do. You know there is something inside of you, some form of expression or creative talent that needs to be channeled, but what? Of course, this is something only you can discover. Once you have, discovering how to effectively learn from and share with those around you is vital to achieving your goal.

Identifying the Passion

In the beginning, Jenai Lane did not know exactly what she wanted to do. She knew she wanted to create a business that was her own. She knew she was creative. She knew she had great imagination and a flair for style. This was the basis of her passion. She wanted to do something more. Can this really be the beginning of a business venture? You better believe it. This is, as Ed Moldt points out, the entrepreneurial spirit. Lane wanted more and was so determined she was ever on the hunt to find her niche. Then, when she discovered how much she enjoyed creating and designing jewelry, a feeling of empowerment came over her: I can do this! Since then she has designed several new products for Respect, Inc., such as the stylish laptop backpack seen here.

Jenai Lane sporting a backpack she designed for her company Respect, Inc.

Debbi Fields knew that she wanted ... more. But what? She went along her day-to-day life, raising her family, and baking cookies — her only passion. Slowly she began to realize what the *more* was. It wasn't a lightening bolt, as Lane experienced, but a gradual awakening. Still, it was a passion. For centuries, women like Lane and Fields wanted more. They felt something was missing.

There is a wonderful poem by Emily Dickinson that expresses that yearning and the limitations of boundaries.

Over the fence —
Strawberries — grow —
I could climb — if I tried, I know —
Berries are nice!
But — if I stained my Apron —
God would certainly scold!
Oh, dear — I guess if He were a Boy —
He'd — climb — if He could!

Emily Dickinson, despite her beauty, creativity, and brilliance, felt confined by her role as woman. Her boundaries were clearly defined, and she dared not move beyond them.

Undoubtedly, Dickinson could have created and written her own business plan; seeing it through to the next stage, however, would have been impossible. Through no fault of her own, she could not. But women of today are empowered. We can have those berries. We can climb the fence and stain our clothes.

Ruth Wakefield is an example of an entrepreneur discovering a passion. In 1930, this wonderful woman changed the face of nighttime munchies forever. It was an important moment in history for all real chocolate lovers. Wakefield owned a hotel in Massachusetts called The Toll House Inn. One afternoon while she prepared to make a batch of Butter Drop Do Cookies for her patrons, she diced up a bar of semi-sweet chocolate and added it to the dough to give it an extra chocolate flavor. The bits of chocolate did not melt as she expected but kept a soft, gooey form within the baked cookies. They were an instant hit with her customers. Because of Wakefield's passion for cooking, her willingness to experiment, and her business experience, she was able to create an empire.

Cris Dolan knew she wanted something more. She was driven. Also, she had passion and tenacity. Dolan knew she wanted to control, organize, and guide a business venture. She didn't wait for something to fall into her lap, but took a variety of classes, talked to different people, listened, and took notes, trying to decide where and how she would move up the corporate ladder. She became a research assistant in the information and entertainment section of the renowned Media Lab at M.I.T., investigating the presentation of personalized news and interactive storytelling. Her thesis explored the future of sports media with digital interactive television. As a student, she served on the M.I.T. Athletics Board and the M.I.T. Corporation Joint Advisory Council. There were no opportunities lying around. Dolan pounced on everything, including the skeleton.

Dolan — entrepreneur and dare-devil — holds a master of computer science engineering and a bachelor's degree in electrical engineering with a minor in business. In her spare time, she competed internationally in skeleton, speeding down mountains at over eighty miles per hour, and was ranked the number one female skeleton racer in the world. But how did that prepare her for being a businesswoman?

Past, present, or future, women who are passionate and determined make indefatigable entrepreneurs, regardless of their background. Passion activated makes things happen.

Networks

After her crowning performance on the international skeleton circuit, Dolan returned to the Olympic Training Center in Lake Placid, New York, on a mountainous high. She was sitting in the cafeteria when an Olympic official told her that her successes were really non-existent, since women's skeleton was still not an official Olympic sport.

As unbelievable as it sounds, women were still unwelcome in the bobsled and skeleton worlds. Dolan's latest achievements served only as a threat that more women would be coming and that corporate funding would have to be shared with the men — it was feared as much as half.

In 1994, Dolan was one of only three female skeleton racers in the nation and the only woman racer at the Olympic Training Center — a lone target for the men's rancor. Conditions improved for her and others when more women stepped into the arena and more funding became available due to their participation.

Encouragement of women by women has been vital to the success of both businesswomen and athletes. In spite of the federal government's leisurely response to providing assistance for women-owned start-up businesses, women have moved forward. In 1998, approximately 8.5 million

Cris Dolan racing on her skeleton down the Lake Placid, New York, track in 1996 women-owned businesses were operating in the United States,[1] but not without the help of many individuals and women's organizations. One thing is very clear: women need to share their successes and failures with each other.

While researching this book, I heard and read several great lines and words of encouragement; but none sounded as sweet as Jenai Lane's sentiment: "I want to create an old girl network." During our second interview, Lane expressed this desire. She had to go it alone when she started her business. She took some hard knocks from other business people and the banking community, but one of the most difficult things for her to comprehend was the counterproductive way some women treated each other.

"I would go to these trade shows and watch women fight for the little bit of power that was thrown our way and think, This is wrong. We need to learn to work together, instead of fighting with each other. We should not view each other as competitors, but encourage each other. You know, it has always been divide and conquer. All people who are oppressed have always been fed that. But it doesn't work. Look at the third world countries. So many different factions fighting against each other all the time. Can you imagine if everyone started working together?"

But where are the networks? How can you get connected to one? Unfortunately, you can't just look them up in the Yellow Pages. A network is described as a group of people who share common ideas or concerns. These people are not necessarily on the same side of the issue and, indeed, may be adversaries. Democrats and Republicans, for example, check with each other to determine what the other side is thinking about an issue or how they will vote. One may exchange information all the time without any further objective than to be sure items of interest are being shared broadly.

When Tara Cronbaugh wanted to own a coffeehouse, she had no idea where to turn or what she needed to do. But when she enrolled in Ed Moldt's entrepreneur class, the networking began. Through Moldt, Cronbaugh met other professors with a common interest in her succeeding who referred her to the business loan office on campus, and when talking with members of the coffee industry, Cronbaugh added more names and telephone numbers to her network.

You don't have to be buddies with everyone in your network. If there are people who are important to your passion, even when you don't particularly like them or they're your competition, it is wise to stay in touch with them. As one business leader puts it, "My life experience is that it is better to know what the other side is thinking, thus better to stay in touch, than to be surprised."

Someone you wouldn't normally associate with may be helpful because it serves his or her interest to do so and vice versa. For example, Sally and Jane are both in the restaurant business. Not only are they rivals, they don't like each other very much. Just the same, Jane calls Sally to warn her the city council is reviewing Sally's adherence to the city health code. Why? Jane believes the director of the city's public health department has been unjustifiably hard on several women in business, so she doesn't want him to succeed in creating hardships for another woman. Possibly, Jane would have called her even if she were not in a network with Sally, but the likelihood is increased if there is a network relationship.

Anyone who is committed to the idea of being a viable networker is assured success, probably in many different networks. Tess Rano was a full-time respiratory therapist and devoted member of the PTA at her children's school. While she trained for her black belt, she also developed strong relationships with those training with her.

When the time came for her to open her own karate school, she not only drew upon those who shared this common interest (those she trained with) but people at the hospital and her children's school. In addition, Tess was able to use her husband's strong network. As an active

Tess Rano leads boxing practice with gusto   member of the Chamber of

Commerce in Westerville, Rick Rano was well connected with many business owners and other members of the community.

Becoming and remaining a viable member of your network is crucial. Fortunately, it has never been easier to network than now. With Internet access to common interest networks and e-mail access to your own networks, you can keep your channels of communication open with anyone and everyone.

Passion and Networks Change the World Around Us

Businesswomen understand and support the process of networking. But hunting down all the celebrities — athletes, actresses, and models —

while working on *The Quiet Storm* and *Entering the MotherZone* was an exhausting experience. Locating individuals wasn't difficult, but the process of going through agents, managers, public relation agents, and assistants drove me to near madness. Interview requests had to be written in such a way that no other celebrity name but the one in question would appear. I was told repeatedly by agents, celebrities do not like to see the names of other celebrities. Agents want their clients to have top billing.

Author at a booksigning for *The Quiet Storm* in a Columbus, Ohio, B. Dalton book store

Businesswomen have a completely different attitude. Locating people for this book was a simple matter of networking. As the list began to build, so did the enthusiasm. These women were excited to hear about the others and to share information concerning needs, accomplishments, challenges, and even disappointments. They were willing to talk about the other side of success — their mistakes, the frustrations of financing start-up costs, their blunders with opening days and hiring staff, and personal set-backs. It was empowering.

The women's organizations found in the Resources section showed great interest in this project. Each organization was truly appreciative of and excited about the idea of drawing more women into the world of business and entrepreneurialism. Many asked the simple yet all-important question, "What more can we do?"

Many women who have fulfilled their greatest passion and become successful in the business world have developed a new passion. Because they were able to succeed at their first love, whether it was baking cookies or designing one of the ten largest Internet providers in the world, these women have been given the opportunity to give back to their communities and to the world. And they have responded with passion.

Mrs. Fields' Cookies, Jenny Craig Weight Management Centers, PowerBar, Inc., and Cheryl&Co. have given several millions of dollars to local and national charities.

Fields stood outside in the pouring rain selling cookies to raise funds for the Cystic Fibrosis Foundation in New York City. She was so caught up in the energy and emotion of the other participants of a ten kilometer run for Cystic Fibrosis, she wound up running the entire race. Never having trained or jogged more than a block, Fields was supposed to open up the races by literally running around the block then dropping out — she was to be merely a show piece. Suddenly, it became very important to her not only run in the race but to finish, and that's precisely what she did.

In recent years, Jenny and Sid Craig have donated $10 million to California State University at Fresno and another $10 million to the University

Jenny Craig relaxing

of San Diego. They continue to give to the United Way and local hospices. As Craig puts it, "What we give, we give personally. We do not like to give through the company because it is a public company. We don't like spending other people's money.

"You hear athletes today say they don't want to be role models, but it is no longer a choice. Because they are successes on their teams, they become role models for all those aspiring to the same success." The same, she says, is true of businesswomen.

Jenai Lane shares the same philosophy. Respect, Inc. gives a percentage of its proceeds to non-profit organizations focusing on local, national, and global issues including AIDS, endangered species, human rights, domestic violence, and children issues. "When I used to work for other people, I thought 'Wouldn't it be great if employers would pay their employees to do volunteer work?' I think most people want to do something to help but they are just too busy. People don't have the time." So Lane made time by paying her employees to work once a month as volunteers for the charities of their choice."

Jennifer Maxwell's company, PowerBar, Inc., was made up of active outdoor enthusiasts, so land conservation was their focal issue. Having witnessed many threats to public land and waterways, Maxwell and PowerBar employees became committed to protecting, preserving, and restoring the gifts Mother Nature has given. Since the program's inception in 1996, PowerBar has donated more than $260,000 in

Jennifer Maxwell enjoying the outdoors on a preserved path with her two golden retrievers

Direct Impact on Rivers and Trails (D.I.R.T.) grants to more than ninety organizations in the United States.

"Getting out onto the many beautiful trails in the San Francisco Bay Area inspired and challenged us during our competitive running careers. Trail runs and hikes continue to be an important part of our family's favorite activities. D.I.R.T. has helped grassroots organizations ensure that trails and waterways remain accessible and properly maintained for public use," says Maxwell. "Providing grants at the local level has allowed us to see positive changes in communities across the country. At PowerBar our goal was to ensure that no one runs out of trail before they run out of energy!"

It is this kind of business philosophy that has *Fortune* and other top business magazine editors talking about a new trend in business practices, a trend that is being led by women entrepreneurs. It is a trend of social consciousness linking business and community.

Networking's Winning Philosophy

No doubt Ed Moldt would identify poet Emily Dickinson as the kind of student he had in mind when he talked about teaching creative artists about the world of business. Dickinson was confined by certain boundaries. She is one of a majority of people who stop short of finding entrepreneurial success because they believe they have certain boundaries that cannot be challenged. Too often women feel threatened by the idea of creating a business plan and get stuck in the fear. Another good idea melts away.

Networking is another extremely important aspect of building a successful business, and learning the art is too often neglected because it requires overcoming boundaries of fear — fear of exposure, rejection, or obligation. But networking actually connects women and broader horizons. Successful people understand the importance of networking. They never fail to get or give a business card, return a phone call or a favor, or follow up an encounter with people they might need or be able to help somewhere down the road. Skilled networkers pay careful attention to people they encounter and use this unique form of communication to benefit others as well as themselves.

An example comes from an experience shared with my father — one of the most diligent networkers alive today. My father is a former U.S. diplomat and Army intelligence officer. He's a war veteran and one of the most widely recognized and decorated military attaches to have served our nation. By 1985, Col. Marc Powe had seen and heard it all — or so he thought. As a former protégé of his, it seems funny to realize, even he had boundaries.

While taking a college communications course, one assignment was to report on the country of Jordan as though I was a citizen. Dad mentioned that Queen Noor was actually an American citizen from Washington D.C. — where we lived at the time — who married the recently deceased King Hussein of Jordan. I might try to approach my report from that angle, he suggested. Too late. My wheels were already turning. I could call Her Majesty and ask her directly.

"Don't be absurd," my dad warned me, barely looking up from his newspaper. "You can't just call the Queen and ask how the weather is." Now, I never consciously redefined my boundaries. I just knew I wanted to take a shot at calling the Queen. How far could I go?

I called the operator and was connected to the international operator. I asked to speak with the operator of Jordan. I heard my father chuckle. "It's ringing," I reported, holding a hand over the receiver. My dad raised an eyebrow. I asked to speak to the palace operator. My father snorted behind his newspaper.

"It's ringing," I said and my dad lowered his newspaper. When a faraway voice answered in Arabic, I asked to speak to someone who spoke English. "It's ringing," I said again, and I sensed my father sit forward a bit. Half a smile was beginning to form as I asked the English-speaking person on the other end of the line if I might speak to the Queen.

"It's ringing," I informed my dad. By now, his newspaper was lying on his lap, completely forgotten. A full-blown smile appeared when I asked to speak to the Queen's assistant, made my way through her personal secretary and another English-speaking person. The man who had seen and heard it all could only shake his head when the Queen answered, and I asked her — oh, this is so embarrassing — "What is the weather like there?" I hadn't prepared for being successful.

Amusing though this story is, there was a good lesson to be learned. Part of the winning philosophy of networking is being prepared, being ready for the possibilities of each and every moment. It is important to be positive and willing to take risks, but you can miss an ideal opportunity if you are not prepared to succeed.

In my case, if I hadn't rushed into the phone calling process, focused on the challenge of simply getting through, I could have learned a bit about her and had a list of questions prepared. I could have benefitted from her kindness rather than wasting her time. Instead, I found myself embarrassed, unprepared, and babbling about the weather. To be honest, much of that short-lived conversation is a blur; however, I will always remember and appreciate her graciousness and her role in my learning such a valuable lesson.

From that time onward, I've been in contact in one way or another with the most amazing array of people simply because I have learned how to benefit from networking — to have respect for the people I encounter and the process — and how to use my beloved telephone. I have no boundaries, thanks to a challenging father and a gracious queen.

Since my telephonic raid on the Jordanian palace, my father has retired from the military and is Head of Security for World Bank, United Nations, and UNICEF. His contacts are worldwide. But, as he points out, whether you are networking as a business leader, sports agent, writer, or peacekeeper, the philosophy is the same: keep contacts alive and share. "You always try to build a relationship, try to establish some common interest, and follow up quickly with an e-mail or phone call. If you are truly a good networker, you can't be selfish. You have to be willing to give to people. My philosophy of good networking comes into play by ending phone calls with the question, 'Is there anything else I can do for you?' It's a sincere question, but it will also engender people to being helpful in return."

Share the Wealth

Jenai Lane, saddened by women fighting over what little power there was to be had at trade shows, wished more women would choose — and learn how — to work together and help each other. It is particularly exciting to participate in that happening. Lane speculates what it would be like if a women's network really got under way and began to assert itself. "Can you imagine if everyone started working together?" she wondered aloud.

When networking, you cannot be selfish. Lane has seen first-hand the destruction and waste of business leaders fighting over power rather than sharing the wealth. Lane lives her belief: in order to grow stronger, you must share. She is a perfect example of a networker who shares her contacts to help others. In fact, she readily shared several good contacts with me. While tracking down several Olympic athletes, I developed a strong networking relationship with many sports agents. There was one in particular who was interested in representing women bobsledders. He had no idea I was once a bobsledder and was once at odds with the bobsled federation. Regardless, a sports agent of his caliber could dramatically improve things for the women's team, so I put him in touch with them. Mindfully using a network to benefit others is key to maintaining your good standing.

Don't Expect Paybacks

Part of sharing in a network requires faith in the importance of being generous and the knowledge that your cup is already half full. I have known many people who calculate their actions for rewards — if I do this, then that will happen. However, as my dear old dad says, "Be generous because it is the natural thing to do. The nice thing about networking in this way is there are very few people in my network whom I would hesitate to call and ask for help. I know if they can help, they will because they know I would do the same for them. As an information gatherer I have learned over the years that the more information I give, the stronger my network gets." In truth, his network is huge and widely regarded.

One reason for this is he has learned to develop different kinds of relationships with different types of contacts. These relationships, which we have identified as Mercantile, Anticipatory, Cold Call, and Terminal, are as complex as any personal relationship. Each one needs to be tended with great care and respect. As you build your business contacts, you may find you can have more than one kind of relationship with some contacts, depending upon your needs. Regardless your needs, remember the importance of maintaining the relationships in your network. Without these relationships you can never achieve the kind of success needed to build a strong and lasting business.

Mercantile

If you have seen the television show M*A*S*H, you'll remember scenes of Radar O'Reily bargaining and bartering for medical supplies and extra goodies. These scenes are not far from real life. My father tells similar stories of his service in Vietnam, when he and soldiers in other units exchanged items they had for items they needed. In one instance, he was in search of extra plywood for his men, so they could build a recreation center out of a shed where they lived temporarily.

Since it was good for morale, he went on the hunt, exchanging extra paint with another Army unit. This is an example of mercantile networking. In the Mercantile system, both parties agree to stay in contact, trading whenever one or the other wants or needs anything. It is a give/give relationship.

Anticipatory

This relationship implies that you foresee a time when you might be able to work with the new contact. When you are networking, you anticipate that you have things others want, and this is understood by both parties involved. This does not mean, however, that both parties have to be active in the relationship. For example, a friend and business acquaintance of mine called wanting to use my Rolodex. He was in search of a capital investor to buy out a company he was interested in. He knew that I had extensive contacts with the kind of people who might be interested in his proposal. Gladly, I turned over some possible contacts that suited his needs, but I did not ask for anything in return. In no way was his contact a threat to me or any of my business ventures, and in no way was I interested in paybacks. At that point, only one party was involved when he used my contacts. I went about my business and wished him luck. This is anticipatory.

One month later, as luck would have it, he called back. He had been unsuccessful in his earlier attempts and offered me a two percent finders fee if I could help him find a investor. Now, both parties are involved, making ours a mercantile relationship.

Cold Call

The cold call relationship can be with a complete stranger or someone you knew before but only now recognize as someone with potential of future contacts. When I called Premier Management and spoke to sports agent, Evan Morganstein, he was a complete stranger. I wanted and needed only one thing from him: Olympic swimmer, Angel Martino's phone number. But as we began to talk, we found we had a lot more in common. One phone call turned into dozens and dozens of e-mail exchanges. The relationship moved from cold call to anticipatory as we began to share information. I introduced him to the world of bobsledding, and he worked a book deal for me to cover Olympic diver Mark Ruiz. From there, we moved to the mercantile relationship as we began collaborating on a sports marketing book, *How to Be a Sports Agent.* We are in constant contact with the understanding we can give and expect something from each other anytime.

Terminal

This last relationship, while not at all uncommon in the business and sports worlds, is difficult to understand. Using sports as an example one more time, you see this mentality frequently. There is always the person on the field who wants to receive the pass but never wants to pass back. The only reason this person continues to get the ball is because the other members of the team know he or she can score. When the primary goal of team members is to win, they tolerate this behavior; but it is always short-lived. The team will have little or nothing to do with this person off the field. Just as in the business world, this kind of selfish behavior can only last for a limited amount of time.

While Cris Dolan was working on an extremely important and delicate project, a fellow worker stole her hard work and much of the credit. This was hard for Dolan to accept, but she just moved on to bigger and better projects. Initially, I was surprised by this action. Knowing Dolan as I do, I thought she would raise the roof to immediately right the wrong. Instead, her faith in the network allowed her to let time deal with the perpetrator, while she got on with her life.

Embracing the true philosophy of networking is imperative for success. With this grand form of communicating, trusting relationships can be formed, mountains can be moved, passion can arise, and dreams can come true. It is said: you are only two or three contacts away from any person you need to know — we are that interconnected. All things are possible. Hey, I chatted with the Queen of Jordan.

Your Potential and Possibilities

You may feel unsure about the potential of your idea, project, or invention as a honest-to-goodness business. Remember, many unusual ventures are successful and can be started in many different ways. Now is a good time to see if you have answered to your satisfaction the questions previously posed. You can use this checklist to determine whether you are ready to convert your idea into a successful business.

Your Business Feasibility Checklist

☐ First and foremost, do you believe in yourself and your idea?

☐ Are you a risk-taker?

☐ Is it appropriate for you and your immediate family?

☐ Are you ready to do a feasibility study, including the soul-searching necessary to make an accurate, viable report?

☐ Are you willing to do a business plan, to put in the kind of research required to bring you the success you deserve?

☐ Can you take constructive criticism and act on it?

☐ Are you fast on your feet, willing to change your way of thinking when best for your endeavor?

☐ Can you work with others?

☐ Are you a team player?

When I spoke with Tara Cronbaugh about her initial foray into the world of business, we both had to snicker. "God, it was so tacky. I just didn't know there was another way." But, for Tara, the feeling was so powerful that it literally steered her into that fated bookstore on her college campus. "It just hit me. I walked in and asked to see the owner. They told me he was out so I asked to leave a message. I wrote on this little piece of paper . . . ugh, it's so embarrassing. I wrote something like, 'Heyyyy, my name is Tara. How would you like to have a coffee shop in your bookstore. Call me." Had he been there in person, she's afraid she might have actually cocked her thumbs like a gun and given him a bang, bang, wink, wink. "That is not the way to begin a business venture," Cronbaugh now laughs.

Cronbaugh, like so many others, felt so confident of the need and was so sure of herself she jumped in with both feet. The mistakes were plentiful, but so were the rewards.

> "Behold the turtle. He makes progress only when he sticks his neck out."
> – James Conant

Since it appears possible to be successful in business while learning along the way, it seems fitting to look at a growing company — from the moment of conception to the production of the actual product and the marketing of it.

Chapter 11

Awakening the Dream

—

I f you can conceive, you can achieve. There is a creative spirit in all of us, but it must be awakened. It is a dream, calling, or challenge that drives successful people to achieve their goals. It is a matter of finding your special niche then having the entrepreneurial spirit and perseverance to begin and build a business.

Like Kristin Penta who imagined herself to be the next Estee Lauder, J'Amy Owens possessed that something special at an early age — kindergarten to be exact. It was during a fire drill that Owens discovered her gift for strategic planning and design. She told a reporter, "I stayed behind and re-arranged the desks for easier access and mobility. The teacher paid me a quarter to sit outside for the rest of the year."

Even though Owens' teacher didn't truly appreciate her conceptual talents, Owens continued to visualize things the way they should be. In later years, she learned to convince others and effectively used the media to promote her skills. Today, Owens is president of The Retail Group, Inc. Her company has developed more than 400 design concepts used internationally by thousands of stores. This group of consultants offers strategic retail solutions to clients, such as Homelife, The Great Outdoors, M&M/Mars Corporation, Disney, Blockbuster Video, Sears, Starbucks, NIKE, McDonald's, and AT&T. Owens has become the master of retail design.

Owens is also willing to share her talents and experiences with companies other than just the *Fortune* 500. It is her creative spirit and innate interest in women that makes Owens willing to take a look at new, up and coming businesses. Thanks to some networking, she did so for Stacey Center even though she was asked right smack in the middle of the holidays. Owens takes the concept of women's networking very seriously. Perhaps she remembers the combination of excitement and fear one feels when starting a new business.

Fear? Owens? How could this incredibly sophisticated, bright, self-assured business leader — dubbed "sales guru to the stars"— ever know self-doubt? She's been a cover girl for all the top business magazines and continues to be in demand by big name clients on reputation alone. But there was a time when Owens didn't know where she was going. It was 1985. Owens had just been fired from a specialty-store chain where, among other things, she oversaw merchandise displays. When Owens noted that some of the stores had in-house security problems and reported it to the higher-ups, she was fired. They had not employed her, they said, to play house detective.

Not knowing what else to do, Owens began working for an architectural firm, taking home ten percent commission on any work she brought in from retail. There was no base salary. Still, within a short time she was making so much money her employers realized she would be making more money than they, so they offered her a salaried position. This was a defining moment for Owens.

It was a moment of revelation in which she realized she knew much more than she thought she did, and that her boundaries did not define her or her capabilities. So, she quit her job and founded The Retail, Inc. This woman with no formal background in business was suddenly telling the most successful businesses in the world how to be more successful. Oh, the irony.

Some ten years later, in 1999, Owens remembers the beginning, as she takes time from her very busy schedule to look at The Soap Quarry, a small one-woman company that just recently appeared on the Internet. Its owner, Stacey Center, created the website while on an extremely restricted budget and with very little inventory in stock.

When I first contacted Center, she was hesitant to talk with me. She was embarrassed. Later, she would confide that she was afraid I would think the whole idea of making soap was silly. The risk-taking phenomena reappears as this ex-ballerina with a Ph.D. in psychology embarks on a business in the soap industry. Does the scenario sound familiar?

Center's story exemplifies the concepts we've been discussing. Each step she took, sometimes conscious, sometimes not, was a move toward success. Center was unaware of Ed Moldt's concept of "defining your boundaries," yet she was able to break free of her boundaries for something she wanted.

"I loved Victorian crafts," Center says. "I don't know why; I just did, and I knew I wanted to try making soap." So Center began finding out what she needed to know. "First, books only talked about making soap from animal fat. My dad's a butcher, so I had access to plenty of animal fat but he told me, 'You don't want to do that because it would be awful,' so I did more research on the Internet, and I learned I could use vegetable oils, instead."

Always looking to release her creative spirit, this former ballet dancer began making soaps and honing her skill as a way to relax. She was holding down a job and preparing for her dissertation. Making soaps, she says, was a way to keep her sanity. As Krueger-Horn, Debbi Fields, and so many other women have said, the business started out as a means of self-expression. However, it became something much more for Center. At one of the most stressful periods in her life, Center also discovered she was pregnant. Almost from the beginning, it was an incredibly difficult pregnancy. The details are still difficult for her to discuss because, in the end, she lost her baby.

Suddenly, there was a terrible void. "I kept making more and more batches, and [husband] Mike said, 'You can't keep doing this. You have

Stacey Center in her kitchen at home mixing up a new batch of soap

to do something with all this.' I had tons of soap." That was when Mike Center suggested the obvious: "Why don't we sell this soap?"

Remember the questions posed earlier: Why am I doing this? How will I do this? What is it that I want? Center was suddenly faced with these questions. With no background in business and nary a clue as to how to start, she turned to the Internet for answers. Remember, we know more than we think we do. In doing research for her dissertation, Center had learned a little about the Internet.

"I taught myself web design for my dissertation because I had my survey online. Finishing a Ph.D. is a good motivator for learning new skills. I learned about creating and marketing, and I was getting awards for that. So when the whole soap business idea came about, it seemed like the thing to do because you don't have to have much of a monetary investment to have an online shop, and it was something I knew I could create. I started writing the web page in September and had it on the Web by the beginning of October. Actually, it was finished before that but we were waiting for our ISP to get ready and reserve the domain name and stuff like that. Finally, *www.soapquarry.com* was actualized.

"After it was set up and I made sure there weren't any broken links or other serious problems with it, I started submitting to search engines — one of the headache aspects of having a webpage store. Search engines are very particular about how they look at your page and where you eventually end up when someone types in a request. I had to study a bit, mostly at the reference sites, to figure out how to configure the pages better, so they could compete with other sites."

One daunting challenge: the keyword, soap. Guess what the top 100 generated choices are, give or take a few? *Soap* operas.

"I still haven't been able to overcome that on some of the engines. There is also a long delay in getting a site listed. Most search engines still haven't referenced the page. Sigh. Next come webrings and awards. These are things that will increase traffic to your site and, indirectly, increase your standing in the search engines, because some of them measure your quality by how many other pages link to you. So, I started researching webrings that might be consistent with the page.

"Also, I started to submit the site for review by some award sites. There are hundreds of these and they fall into categories of Very Difficult, such as Cool Site of the Week, to the Everybody-Wins type of awards. The two awards I got came from an automatic Submit-Your-Site awards service. I was really happy when I searched the index and found out both of the awards are rated at four-out-of-five in terms of difficulty to get."

While Center created her web page, she also created her own feasibility report. Although she had no idea of how to create a Moldt-model feasibility report, she knew instinctively what questions to ask herself.

- What is it I want?
- Is this idea new or fresh enough to generate interest?
- Is it financially feasible?

Center went to the city courthouse and filed for a business license. She filled out the appropriate papers, all of which she reports were relatively easy and painless, and mailed them off with her payments of the fees. She spent less than $100 in the process.

"I didn't know about any feasibility report," Center laughs. "We did a mission statement for our own peace of mind. We needed the lowest costs possible because we are both still paying off school loans. I really thought if I went to a bank they would just laugh. Who makes soap?! But handmade soap is different. Store-bought soaps use detergents. Still, I was really embarrassed about that. Who makes soap?" Who would buy a soft, chewy cookie? Who would buy a Miracle Mop?

Also, Center discovered the importance of what Moldt described as angel networking. A family friend loaned her $1,000 to buy the initial supplies. "It was a personal loan that he has told me I could pay back when I could." Like Gretchen Leddy, avoiding the banks made Center's entrance into the business world much easier.

"I'm sort of entering stage two in my conceptualization of the business," Center says. "I have the initial documents I need to start the business, and basically, I have my initial inventory. I would love to have more, but since I'm operating on a tight budget, I have to wait.

"I've come to realize that a web store isn't like some people think: build it, and they will come. That is a good fantasy. Mine has been up for three months, and I am still generally getting an average of ten hits a day, some of which are friends and family, occasionally just seeing what I'm up to although sometimes they order, too. I haven't actually had a complete stranger, who doesn't know me or Mike, order yet. I think that is a milestone I need to pass. Once the search engines list me, I think traffic will increase somewhat. I'm also counting on word of mouth; and hopefully, when friends buy my things as gifts, the people they give them to will be return customers."

Location was not an issue for Center. As a virtual store, she did not have to worry about renting or leasing. She could easily absolve all business costs, if necessary; but, as Terry Neece warns, getting involved is imperative to success. Neece was too busy to read about local current affairs, so she was unaware of proposed highway construction when she purchased her office only three blocks away. Valerie Coolidge was not aware of the liquor laws regarding cakes before she started her business.

Center did two important things. She found a group of women on the Internet who make and sell soap at craft shows who became her support base, and she researched every aspect of her proposed products and business. Center was quick to follow the experts' advice. She found her mentors and a support group before she began her venture. She had a network. Fields, Mastroianni, and many others could have avoided many problems if they had had this kind of support group. Because she was able to find the group, Center has learned a lot about the process of making, packaging, and selling her products.

"The great thing about these women is all the advice they have given me. Some do craft shows, others own shops. They've helped me with pricing, retail costs, insurance, as well as helping with various herbs, and discovering new properties and bath blends. They have all been so open about sharing ideas."

As Ed Moldt encourages, "Gather as much information as possible. Talk with business people, and be sure to ask the question: What would you do if you were me?"

Tara Cronbaugh poured over trade magazines, learning all the different kinds of coffee blends and flavors; then she educated her pallet to be able to differentiate between them. Lynette Reed educated and trained herself to make scented and blended candles. Center is no different. Her knowledge of all the different kinds of natural herbs and spices is dizzying. She can tell you what exfoliates, hydrates, and smooths the skin. She can tell you that a ginger bath, for example, is not recommended for people with high blood pressure and some other health conditions. She can tell you that it is the acid in tomatoes that can act like a toner. Because of her extensive research, Center saved herself some headaches that might not have been avoided had she not been so vigilant.

Ginger, for example, is reputed to be good for people with diabetes, and it tends to increase the blood circulation; however, to make such

claims one would have to register with the Food and Drug Administration. In addition, FDA regulations would have to be adhered to before she could make any cosmetic claims. Bubble bath was something else Center researched. Because so many women can suffer from yeast infections as a result of warm baths, the FDA regulations for bubble

Ginger Bar soaps

bath manufacturers are extremely strict. "You have to send in the formula and have it independently tested. Anything that can mold must be tested for public safety." By downloading and studying the FDA regulations, Center has avoided a date in court similar to the one Fields suffered. As the judge told Fields all those years ago, it is essential to learn the rules of the game if you are going to play for keeps.

Lavender Melt soaps

Center knows there's a lot more she must learn. "One problem I have is that I understand the web world enough to get along, but I don't have a clue about marketing in the real world. I mean, personally, I loved the J. Peterman catalog. That was my absolute favorite for years. I read the thing when I didn't have enough money to even buy a scarf from that company. I think that is sort of the model I'm using. Never mind that they recently went bankrupt. I think the movie stuff was a

mistake their company made. I mean, how many people can afford the actual dress from *The Titanic*? But I liked the idea that the advertisements could draw people in so that they wanted to read all about them. If you can put a bit of fantasy in, then all the better. With my catalog, soap is cheap enough that people can afford the fantasy."

Calendula Melt soaps

Center's fantasy and passion is in her mission statement and is the company motto, "Pampering yourself doesn't have to cost a fortune." Center wants the world to experience the high quality of her products. Her soaps are an extension of herself. But the question remains, how to build a customer base outside the Internet. With no marketing budget to speak of, Center is aware of the fact that only a small portion of the population shops by way of the Web.

A bar of le Fleur soap. What better way to pamper yourself?

"So there is a ninety-five percentile out there I am not reaching."

Enter J'Amy Owens. "This is a virtual store and she [Center] has the need for people to discover the store outside the Internet without a budget. This is a very tricky proposition. The only way to reach people is obviously, through advertising, word of mouth, creative marketing, and PR, some of which you can do on your own, all of which without a budget takes time. A lot of time. So it is really a question of creative guerrilla marketing and word of mouth and doing things that are based at zero cost. This is a very, very dodgy and precarious way to try to launch a business, so I would say she is behind the eight ball in terms of being able to succeed, and raising capital is the best avenue for her to advance her cause."

There are a variety of possibilities Center can take advantage of to further her cause of raising capital. Jenai Lane found courses provided to economically challenged women for starting up a business. You can find several organizations for women in the Resources section and through your local Chamber of Commerce. However, Owens hit upon a course of action many businesswomen either are unaware of or overlook in the initial stages of their business careers: creative guerrilla marketing.

Reminiscent of the stories of Lynette Reed, Diane Jacobs, Cozy Wolan, and others, Center set out to promote herself with high profile customers. She chose twenty big-name celebrities, contacting their publicists and offering free samples from The Soap Quarry. A friend with public relations experience contacted the local paper, and some widely circulated publications about the award-winning Center's soap-making talent. It proved to be a human interest piece that several of them were interested in.

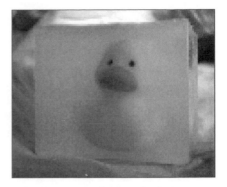

Center also adopted the strategy used by Cecilia "Pudge" Kleinkauf. By creating a mailing list compiled by a computer company, Center will be able to target a large female audience. According to Owens, as

Who can resist this Ducky little soap

long as one is committed to doing creative guerrilla and word-of-mouth marketing at zero cost, the effort can be effective. But emphasis must be placed on commitment, full-time commitment.

Particularly painful for the quiet, soft-spoken Center, was developing the art of selling herself. While she relied on family members and friends to start the ball rolling, it was ultimately Center who spoke with the press, conducted interviews, and sold herself and her product.

All of the women in this book, including Center are also part of something vital to us all. By selling herself and her ideas and telling her story, she is becoming part of a women's network. The art of selling oneself is difficult for many women, but if you truly believe in your idea or product, it is easier.

"In this life, you must do your best to find work you can invest in with personal passion," says Internet pioneer Isabel Maxwell. She should know, as the president of Commtouch, the world's leading provider of 'branded e-mail,' Maxwell knows all about the fine art of communication and selling. In fact, it was less than a decade ago Maxwell didn't even understand how to use Internet guides much less run a million dollar on-line service.[1]

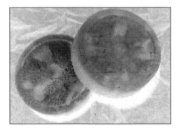

Owens cautions, "My first piece of advice would be, 'Don't quit your day job.' If you can stand working your day job while starting up your own business, if you can work around the clock, you will know if you've got what it takes to be an entrepreneur. This is a tough way of life." It was

Loofa Glycerin soap

said over and over again, in the beginning not one had any idea of how many hours would be dedicated to their businesses. Nor did any foresee their businesses would become all-consuming, taking up precious family time, swallowing relationships whole, and leaving very little time for anything else.

Jenny Craig asks hopeful businesswomen, "What is it you will have to give up to make the business successful?" She warns that something will have to give and asks again, "Are you willing to make that sacrifice in the name of your business?"

"I can spend hours making my soaps and not even notice that all those hours are gone," Center responds. Her business has complimented her life beautifully. Married to a man who travels often, it is easy for her to let The Soap Quarry be her companion. But what will happen when she has a family and the needs of her baby pull her away from deadlines and big orders? We have seen from Lynette Reed, Tara Cronbaugh, and many other successful mothers, it is possible to do both. The question, as to whether you are prepared to make the sacrifices your business will demand of you, remains for you to answer.

"The pay off is worth it," says Owens. "Be willing to crawl over broken glass. Somewhere there is going to be a crack that will get you your opening. If you can't get through the front door, try the back, the side, anything. Fortitude really counts here. More than brains, it is who is the most willing and persistent."

The Real Deal

I received an e-mail from Center a few weeks into our interviews. It read simply: "Just received my first order from a complete stranger. Here we go." Although I could only stare at the words on a cold screen, I imagined the excitement she must be feeling. Just a few days earlier, when asked to name her strengths and weaknesses as an entrepreneur, she laughed about her response about her strengths. "I never had the formal training. I don't know enough to be afraid." This was precisely what Fields cited as a positive for her. In other words, they were not and are not defined by boundaries.

Because Center has not been defined by these boundaries, her possibilities seem endless. Unlike some other businesses, The Soap Quarry makes a perfect model. Its creator found a passion, an extension of herself she wanted to share with others. And, while money is a long-term goal, it was never her motivating factor.

Center, like Wolan and Krueger-Horn, continued to work her day job while logging hours and hours into research, fine-tuning, and re-tuning her mission statement and web page. She became involved with a support and mentoring group and began asking all the right questions. By immediately contacting the FDA and gathering still more information, she avoided any legal problems. Center found out the rules of the game before she began to play.

Her business was set up in a way in which absolving all costs and getting out the back door could be done quickly and easily. Then, as Owens suggested, Center began her marketing strategy on a local, national, and international level. How was it international? By creating a website then contacting award sites for review, not only did Center win two noteworthy awards, but she caught the attention of other companies in the soap business, including an international company that would later negotiate to align itself with The Soap Quarry.

Center adopted the marketing approach that Owens identifies as "Inclusion" (described in Chapter 7) to appeal to her customers. By reading about her soaps in the way J. Petermen presented merchandise, Center's customers feel a sense of membership with The Soap Quarry. Similar to Fields, Center bases her company's mission around making her customers happy.

"We understand that some individuals will have preferences or special needs. You can come to The Soap Quarry and get anything you want. Anybody can make a request. If they want personal attention, that is what I am here for."

A job worth doing . . . . How does that go?

Center thinks fast on her feet, a requirement Moldt says is imperative for a successful entrepreneur. Center is willing to change directions at the drop of a hat for the good of The Soap Quarry. Of course, this is the same woman who would throw away an entire batch because she didn't like the slightly faded color or texture of the soap. This demand for perfection is, in fact, very similar to that of Fields. The Fields name and her product meant much more to her than the cost. It is this same kind of perfectionism in Center that caught the eye of an international company, Adaptation Software.

"When I first started the company, I know there were people who thought, 'Why is she spending so much time on the web design?'" Center says, "I know this is something I could have gotten a friend or college student to do for a small fee, but I felt like I had to learn every aspect of the business. I mean, if I was going to have an online shop, it was something I should and could create."

Because Center insisted on learning all the rules, including how to create her own website, unexpected opportunities came her way. Adaptation Software, a United Kingdom-based company, wanted Center to work as a web designer for them. Here comes the good part. Adaptation Software also owns O'Natural, another U.K.-based company that sells cosmetics and soaps. O'Natural is a large cosmetic company in the U.K. and Middle East that supplies spas with various soaps and toiletries in Spain, the United Kingdom, Oman, and Jordan. With more than 160 commercial customers, O'Natural is interested in the soap business and, more specifically, The Soap Quarry. After only six months in operation, but far too many hours to count, negotiations were under way to make The Soap Quarry a sister company to O'Natural.

Instead of moving to the United Kingdom, however, Center, who is expecting her second child, decided to expand in the U.S. market with a plan to go international in five years. In addition, she has been asked by a group called Organics Made Easy to create an exclusive line for them. Like Lynette Reed, Center is learning how to produce and market her products under different names to satisfy a variety of customers.

As our interviews came to a close, I browsed through the guestbook page Center created on her website. There I discovered the words of customer Erica Dufrene of LaPlace, Louisianna. Never was something more aptly put. She wrote: "Cheers for the entrepreneur!"

And for their passion.

Passion — faith's companion — can move mountains, and there is no greater passion than that of a woman. With passion, you, too, can develop a successful business and a successful you.

Endnotes

Introduction

1. Pamela Gilberd, *The Eleven Commandments of Wildly Successful Women,* Macmillan Spectrum, U.S.A., 1996; p. xi.

2. Michelle Spillan, "Rising Stars," Columbus *CEO* (July 1998), p. 16.

3. Pamela Gilberd, *The Eleven Commandments of Wildly Successful Women,* Macmillan Spectrum, U.S.A., 1996; p. 84.

Chapter 1

1. "Should You Join the Millions of Successful Women Home Entrepreneurs?" *Wealth Building* (May 1997), p. 6.

2. "Reality Check," *Working Woman* (July 1998), p. 33.

Chapter 2

1. *People,* (November 30, 1998), p. 97.

2. Kate White, *Why Good Girls Don't Get Ahead ... But Gutsy Girls Do,* Warner Books, New York, N.Y., 1995.

3. Alexandra Powe Allred and Michelle Powe, *The Quiet Storm,* Masters Press, Indianapolis, Indiana; p. 47.

4. Nicola Godfrey, "Just B.," *Working Woman* (November 1998), p. 30.

5. *People* (December 14, 1998), p. 99.

Chapter 3

1. Debbi Fields, *One Smart Cookie,* Simon & Schuster, N.Y., 1987; p. 63.
2. Cynthia E. Griffin, "Brave New World," *Entrepreneur Magazine* (April 1999), p. 49.

Chapter 5

1. Liedtke, Michael, "Venture Capitalists Ignoring Businesses Owned by Women," *Columbus Dispatch*, (July 18, 2000); Bus E1.
2. Bob Weinstein, "Let Us Count the Ways," *Entrepreneur Magazine* (April 1999), p. 168A.

Chapter 6

1. Deborah Swiss, *Women Breaking Through: Overcoming the Final 10 Obstacles at Work*, Peterson's/Pacesetter Books, Princeton, N.J., p. 59.
2. Entrepreneur Woman: "Fighting Discrimination and More," *Entrepreneur Magazine* (September 1997), p. 57.
3. Pamela Gilberd, *The Eleven Commandments of Wildly Successful Women*, Macmillan Spectrum, U.S.A., 1996; p. 84.

Chapter 7

1. Kate White, *Why Good Girls Don't Get Ahead . . . But Gutsy Girls Do*, Warner Books, New York, N.Y., 1995.
2. Edward O. Welles, "The Diva of Retail," *Inc.* (October 1999), p. 38.
3. Nicola Godfrey, "Just B," *Working Woman Magazine* (April 1999), p. 30.
4. Robert McGarvey, "Fun and Games," *Entrepreneur Magazine* (April 1999), p. 83.

Chapter 10

1. "Woman's World," *Entrepreneur Magazine* (January 1999), p. 23.

Chapter 11

1. Ben-David, Calev, *Working Woman* (May 2000), p. 76.

Resources:
Organizations

American Association of University Women
  for Fellowships and Grant Programs
AAUW Educational Foundation
P.O. Box 4030
Iowa City, IA 52243-4030
Phone: (319) 337-1716

The AAUW is a membership organization that promotes equity and education for all women and girls, lifelong education, and positive societal changes. The AAUW Fellowships and Grant Programs offers educational opportunities to entrepreneurial hopefuls.

American Business Women's Association (ABWA)
9100 Ward Parkway
Kansas City, MO 64114-0728
Phone: (816) 361-6621 or (800) 228-0007
FAX: (816) 361-4991
Internet: www.abwa.org

ABWA's mission is to provide opportunities that help women survive and thrive in the workplace and grow personally and professionally through leadership, education, networking support, and national recognition.

American Society of Women Accountants (ASWA)
60 Revere Drive, Suite 500
Northbrook, IL 60062
Phone: (800) 326-2163 or (847) 205-1029   (continued)

American Society of Women Accountants (ASWA)   (continued)
FAX: (847) 480-9282
e-mail: aswa@aswa.org
Internet: www.aswa.org

The ASWA is a personal and professional network of successful professionals who understand the unique challenges of being a woman in the workplace. ASWA membership is available to individuals in all areas of accounting and finance including public accounting, private industry, non-profit groups, government agencies, and academia looking to hone leadership and management skills and develop strong network and mentoring systems.

American Women's Economic Development Corporation (AWED)
216 E. 45th Street, 10th Floor
New York, NY 10017
Phone: (917) 368-6100
FAX: (212) 986-7114

AWED is designed to help the hopeful entrepreneur with virtually every aspect of business development — from start-up to growth. AWED provides women with the training needed to get started, manage a business, and seek expansion capital. Individual business assessments are conducted by counselors who will make recommendations about what your business will need and how to meet new challenges.

Association of Black Entrepreneurs (ABWE)
P.O. Box 49368
Los Angeles, CA 90049
Phone: (213) 624-8639

ABWE targets business and educational support and assistance for black women entrepreneurs, as well as women (and men) interested in business networking and referrals.

Association for Women in Computing (AWC)
41 Sutter Street, Suite 1006
San Francisco, CA 94104
Phone: (415) 905-4663
E-mail: awc@awc-hq.org
Internet: www.awc-hq.org

AWC was founded in 1978 with the mission of promoting the advancement of women in computing professions. This is a not-for-profit organization for all women interested in information and/or networking in the field of technology.

Business Women's Network (BWN)
1146 19th Street, 3rd Floor
Washington, DC 20036
Phone: (800) 48WOMEN
FAX: (202) 833-1808
Internet: www.bwni.com

The Business Women's Network's mission is to empower women and professional women by providing networking and marketing skills, educational opportunities, resources and a strong mentoring program.

Chamber of Commerce of the United States
1615 H Street NW
Washington D.C. 20036
Phone: (202) 659-6000
FAX: (202) 463-5836
Internet: www.uschamber.com

The U.S. Chamber of Commerce is the world's largest business federation. It provides research, statistical information, and survey services that can enhance the operations and profitability of your business or organization. The U.S. Chamber of Commerce offers training tools and products developed to advance and support business and enhance their ability to promote free enterprise. As a member to this organization, you may exercise your voice on Capitol Hill.

Child Care Action Campaign (CCAC)
330 7th Avenue, 14th Floor
New York, NY 10001
Phone: (212) 239-0138
FAX: (212) 268-6515
E-mail: info@childcareaction.org

The CCAC's campaign is to increase investment in child care so that all children can develop to their fullest potential and families can get and keep jobs. CCAC engages leaders in education and business to improve the quality of child care and early education. CCAC communicates child care trends, research, legislation, and program innovations to national audiences and provides expert opinion to the media. CCAC is an excellent source for the working mother.

Direct Marketing Association (DMA)
1120 Avenue of the Americas
New York, NY 10036
Phone: (212) 768-7277
FAX: (212) 768-4547
Internet: www.the-dma.org   (continued)

Direct Marketing Association (DMA)　(continued)

The DMA is a membership based organization that offers the latest information in marketing, including teleservices, Internet services, and postal reform. The DMA has chapters on national and international levels, bringing marketing information to Latin and North America, Asia, and Europe.

Executive Women International
515 South 700 East, Suite 2A
Salt Lake City, UT 84102
Phone: (801) 355-2800
　　　1 (888) EWI-1229 (toll free)
FAX: (801) 355-2852
E-mail: ewi@executivewomen.org
Internet: www.executivewomen.org

EWI was established in 1938 as an association of key women working to promote their firms and improve their communities. Over 3,500 companies and 5,000 representatives are members of EWI which has 85 chapters located in major cities in the United States, Canada, and Europe. EWI is the premier organization for networking and leadership development for today's professional businesswomen and their firms.

Independent Small Business Employers of America
520 South Pierce Street, Suite 224
Mason City, Iowa 50401
Phone: (800) 728-3187 or (515) 424-1673

Employers of America makes life easier for employers, managers, and supervisors by providing members with information, guidance, and leadership tools to deal successfully and efficiently with their employees.

Institution of Women's Policy Research (IWPR)
1707 L Street NW, Suite 750
Washington, DC 20036
Phone: (202) 785-5100
FAX: (202) 833-4362
Internet: www.iwpr.org

IWPR is a public policy research organization dedicate to informing and stimulating the debate on public policy issues of critical importance to women and their families. IWPR focuses on issues of poverty and welfare, employment and earnings, work and family, the economic and social aspects of health care and domestic violence, and women's civic and political participation. IWPR is a non-profit organization that works with policymakers, interest groups and graduate programs in public policy and women's studies at The George Washington University.

The International Alliance (TIA)
P.O. Box 1119
Sparks-Glencoe
Baltimore, MD 21152-1119
Phone: (410) 472-4221
FAX: (410) 472-2920
Internet: www.t-i-a.com

The International Alliance, founded in 1980, is a global umbrella organization that connects, supports, and promotes professional, executive, and entrepreneurial women and their networks.

International Association of Business Communicators (IABC)
One Hallidie Plaza, Suite 600
San Francisco, CA 94102
Phone: (415) 544-4700
FAX: (415) 544-4747
Internet: www.iabc.com

IABC is a membership based organization that offers expert advice, step by-step instruction, case studies and proven models for developing strategic communications management. You will learn about reputation management on the net, e-business communities, and managing virtual business relationships. Learn to manage today's communication — communication that is strategic, interactive, integrated, and international.

International Franchise Association (IFA)
1350 New York Avenue NW
Washington, DC 20005
Phone: (202) 628-8000
FAX: (202) 628-0812
Internet: www.franchise.org

The IFA is the best information source for high quality products, professional services, and professional and legal information.

Minority Business Entrepreneur (MBE)
3528 Torrance Boulevard, Suite 101
Torrance, CA 90503-4803
Phone: (310) 540-9398
FAX: (310) 792-8263
E-mail: mbewbw@ix.netcom.com
Internet: www.mbemag.com

The MBE believes the development of minority and women owned businesses to be the cornerstone of building strong, healthy communities in which each individual has the opportunity to contribute, to his or her fullest potential. MBE informs by reporting on issues critical to the growth and development of minority and women owned firms as well as educating them on business development legislation. MBE also profiles successful entrepreneurs and serves as a great mentoring program.

Ms. Foundation for Women
120 Wall Street, 33rd Floor
New York, NY 10005
Phone: (212) 742-2300
FAX: (212) 742-1653
FAX-on-demand service: 1 (800) 809-8206
e-mail: msfdn@interport.net
Internet: www.ms.foundation.org

The Ms. Foundation for Women, the national women's fund, has supported the efforts of women and girls to govern their own lives for more than
25 years. Creator of the "Take Our Daughters to Work Day" program, the
Ms. Foundation funds cutting-edge projects that gives girls the skills they
need to become leaders of tomorrow and provides low-income women with
the tools to lift themselves and their families toward self-sufficiency. For
more information about their services contact their website (above).

National Association for Female Executives, Inc. (NAFE)
135 West 50th Street, 16th Floor
New York, NY 10020
Phone: (212) 445-6235
FAX: (212) 445-6228
Internet: www.nafe.com

Founded in 1972, the National Association for Female Executives is the
nation's oldest and largest businesswomen's association with nearly 150,000
members, including 30,000 women business owners, and 200 networks
worldwide. NAFE provides quality benefits, resources, and services through
education, networking, and public advocacy, to empower its members to
achieve career success and financial security. Whether you want to fine-tune
your management skills or review your career options, NAFE can offer you
the kind of support you need to succeed in business.

National Association of Women Business Owners (NAWBO)
1100 Wayne Avenue, Suite 830
Silver Spring, MD 20910
Phone: (301) 608-2590
FAX: (301) 608-2596
Internet: www.nawbo.org

For more than 25 years members of NAWBO have benefited from its
growing network, advocacy, and available resources. NAWBO offers its
members strong mentoring programs in getting started with extensive research in its library. NAWBO and its members are strong business leaders in
the business community as well as the public policy arena.

National Business Association (NBA)
5151 Beltline Road, Suite 1150
Dallas, Texas 75240
Phone: (972) 458-0900 or (800) 456-0440 (toll free)
FAX: (972) 960-9149
Internet: www.nationalbusiness.org

The National Business Association is a non-profit organization offering services and benefits to the self-employed and small business community.

National Chamber of Commerce for Women
10 Waterside Plaza, Suite 6H
New York, NY 10010
Phone: (212) 685-3454
FAX: (212) 685-4547
E-mail: commerceforwomen@compuserve.com

The NCCW's goal is to help women make gains in business ownership. In creating employment-and-enterprise opportunities for women, the NCCW works with the Small Business Administration, the Library of Congress Referral Center, the Family Impact Seminar, job banks and business incubators. A great networking source.

National Education Center for Women in Business (NECWB)
Seton Hill College
Seton Hill Drive
Greensburg, PA 15601-1599
Phone: (724) 830-4625 or (800) 632-9248 (toll free)
FAX: (724) 834-7131
E-mail: info@setonhill.edu
Internet:www.necwb.setonhill.edu

The mission of the NECWB is to enable the economic self-sufficiency of women through advocacy and educational initiatives in entrepreneurship.

National Federation of Black Women Business Owners (NFBWB)
1500 Massachusetts Avenue, Suite 34
Washington, DC 20005
Phone: (202) 833-3450
FAX: (202) 331-7822
Internet: www.NFBWBO.org

The National Federation of Black Women Business Owners was formed in 1984 with the mission to help women in business who are discriminated against by non-minorities and men, to enable these women to network, build business alliances and acquire loans. The NFBWB is a membership based organization to help women gain access to capital funding, networking and proper training so that they might flourish in the business world.

National Federation of Business and Professional Women's Clubs, Inc.
 of the United States of America (BPW/USA)
2012 Massachusetts Avenue NW
Washington, DC 20036
Phone: (202) 293-1100
FAX: (202) 861-0298
Internet: www.bpwusa.org

The Business and Professional Women's Foundation promotes equity for working women through education, information, and research. The foundation provides financial assistance to women seeking education to advance in their careers or reenter the workforce. The foundation also collects, conducts, and analyzes research on issues affecting women in the work place.

National Federation of Independent Business (NFIB)
600 Maryland Avenue SW, Suite 700
Washington, DC 20024
Phone: (202) 554-9000
FAX: (202) 554-0496
Internet: www.nfib.com

The NFIB is the largest advocacy organization representing small and independent business in the United States. A united community of 600,000 business owners, who employ more than seven million people, make NFIB a powerful association. NFIB works hard with public policy makers and remain true to their mission in advancing the concerns of small business owners among state and federal legislators and regulators.

National Federation for Women Business Owners (NFWBO)
1411 K Street, NW, Suite 1350
Washington, DC 20005-3407
Phone: (202) 638-3060
FAX: (202) 638-3064
E-mail: NFWBO@worldnet.att.net
Internet: www.nfwbo.org

NFWBO, a non-profit research organization, is the premier source of information on women business owners worldwide. Its mission is to support the growth of women business owners by conducting research, sharing information and education. The NFWBO offers research to document the economic and social contributions of women-owned firms, provides consulting and public relations services, and mentors growing businesses. NFWBO leads the way in educating corporations, government policy makers, educators, organizations, the media, and individuals on the importance of supporting women business owners.

National Organization for Women (NOW)
733 15th Street NW, 2nd Floor
Washington, DC 20005
Phone: (202) 331-0066
FAX: (202) 785-8576
Internet: nowfoundation.org
E-mail: Now@now.org

NOW is a membership based organization devoted to furthering
women's rights through education and litigation. NOW is the largest
women's rights organization in the United States, with a membership of
over 500,000 contributing women and men in more than 550 chapters
in all 50 states and the District of Columbia.

Office of Women's Business Ownership
U.S. Small Business Administration
409 3rd Street SW, 4th Floor
Washington, DC 20416
Phone: (202) 205-6673
FAX: (202) 205-7287
WEBMASTER www@www.sbaonline.sba.gov
Internet: www.sba.gov/womeninbusiness
        http://www.sba.gov

The SBA's programs and services can assist you in almost every aspect
of starting your business, from developing a business plan to obtaining
finances, and from marketing your products and services to managing your
company. By using classes and programs on the SBA's World Wide Web site,
and using SBA local services, such as counseling provided through members
of the Service Corps of Retired Executives, you can avoid the common mistakes of business start-ups.

U.S. Small Business Administration: SBA Answer Desk
200 North College Street, Suite A 2015
Charlotte, NC 28202
Phone: 1 (800) UASK SBA
Internet: www.sba.gov

The U.S. Small Business Administration, established in 1953, provides financial, technical, and management assistance to help Americans start, run,
and grow their businesses. With a portfolio of business loans, loan guaran-
tees, and disaster loans worth more than $45 billion, in addition to a venture
capital portfolio of $13 billion, SBA is the nation's largest single financial
backer of small businesses.

Wellesley College Center for Research on Women
106 Central Street
Wellesley, MA 02481-8203
Phone: (781) 283-2500
FAX: (781) 283-2504
Internet: www.wellesley.edu/WCW/index.html

For more than 20 years the Center for Research on Women has been in the forefront of research in which the central questions are shaped by the experiences and perspectives of women. This center offers extensive research, programs, and publications which examine the lives of women, men and children. The Center for Research on Women is an excellent tool for mentoring, business referral, and public policy information.

The White House Office of Women's Initiatives and Outreach
The White House
Room 15 OEOB
Washington, DC 20502
Phone: (202) 456-7300
FAX: (202) 456-7311
Internet: www.whitehouse.gov/women
E-mail: Women's_Office@who.eop.gov

The Clinton administration created the White House Office for Women's Initiatives and Outreach in 1995 to better serve and listen to his constituents. The office serves as a liaison between the White House and women's organizations, listening to women's concerns and proposals and bringing these ideas to the President and others in the Administration.

Women Employed
111 N. Wabash, Suite 1300
Chicago, IL 60602-2002
Phone: (312) 782-3902
FAX: (312) 782-5249

Since 1973, Women Employed has been a leader in the historic drive to open employment opportunities for women. Provides innovative career development and employment services to support women and girls in pursuing their goals. Includes access to training, education, and child care options.

Women in Franchising (WIF)
53 West Jackson Street, Suite 205
Chicago, IL 60604
Phone: (312) 431-1467 or 1 (800) 222-4943 (toll free)
Internet: infonews.com/franchise/wif

Women in Franchising (WIF)   (continued)

Established in 1987, WIF provides franchise consulting services for women and minorities interested in becoming either franchisees or franchisors. National seminar series on audio-cassettes with companion workbooks includes: 1) *Buying a Franchise: How to Make the Right Choice* and 2) *Growing Your Business – the Franchise Option* (the package costs $49.95 plus $5.00 S&H). Consults with franchisors interested in public relations to recruit women and minorities as franchisees. Compiles data on the number of women and minority franchisees. Contractor to the United States Small Business Administration (SBA).

Women Presidents' Organization
598 Broadway, 6th Floor
New York, NY 10012
Phone (212) 941-8510
FAX: (212) 941-9575
E-mail: Wpo1999@aol.com
Internet: www.womenpresidentsorg.com

The Women Presidents' Organization is an exclusive professional development and peer advisory group for successful entrepreneurial women. Each WRO member has already met the challenge of guiding a business to at least $2 million in annual sales (if product driven), or $1 million (if service driven). "She's already proven herself in the still male-dominated business world." Meetings are conducted and coordinated by a professional facilitator with the idea of brainstorming for business development and friendship with fellow magnates.

Women's Business Development Center (WBDC)
8 South Michigan Avenue, Suite 400
Chicago, IL 60603
Phone: (312) 853-3477
FAX: (312) 853-0145
E-mail: WBDCCIED@aol.com

Women's Business Development Center (WBDC) is a not-for-profit organization that offers individualized technical assistance, one-on-one counseling, entrepreneurial training, access to financial technical assistance and credit, and access to Women's Business Enterprise certification and procurement opportunities.

Women's Economic Roundtable (WERT)
1633 Broadway, 35th Floor
New York, NY 10019
Phone: (212) 492-4439
FAX: (212) 492-4436   (continued)

Women's Economic Roundtable (WERT) (continued)

A non-profit educational organization, WERT provides a forum to educate men and women and to inform policy makers about national and global economics, business, and finance. These forums allow us to learn about issues affecting our personal lives, businesses, communities, and the nation. Heavy networking system with business leaders, major corporations, financial institutions, universities, governmental agencies, and the media.

Women's Work Force Network of Wider Opportunities for Women (WOW)
815 15th Street NW
Washington, DC 20005
Phone: (202) 638-3143
FAX: (202) 638-4885

WOW works nationally and in its home community of Washington, D.C. to achieve economic independence and equality of opportunity for women and girls. WOW helps women learn to earn, with programs emphasizing literacy, technical and nontraditional skills, the welfare-to-work transition and career development.

Young Entrepreneurs' Organization
8260 Greensborough Drive, Suite 260
McLean, VA 22102
Phone: (703) 893-5343 or (800) 929-3165 (toll free)
FAX: (703) 893-5222
Internet: www.yeo.org

The YEO is a non-profit educational organization for young entrepreneurs that helps its members build upon their successes through educational and networking opportunities. YEO provides its members access to a great network of peers on an international level.

Young Presidents' Organization (YPO)
451 South Decker Drive
Irving, TX 75062
Phone: (972) 650-4600 or (800) 773-7976 (toll free)
FAX: (972) 650-4777
Internet: www.ypo.org

YPO members include some of the world's most influential corporate and organizational presidents and CEOs. This membership-based organization connects company leaders for peer relationships, mentoring, education, and idea sharing on business, professional, and personal issues.

Resources:
Publications

———

Each of the books mentioned below can help you in one or several areas of your business, from conception, through planning and business plan preparation, to opening and operating your business. These books, available through The Oasis Press, are a part of the Successful Business Library.

Planning Your Business

Before You Go into Business Read This by Ira N. Nottonson
> Explains the basics of business through examples and easy-to-understand language.

Business Owner's Guide to Accounting and Bookkeeping by José Placentia, Bruce Welge, and Don Oliver
> Features clearly written, step-by-step instructions and practice situations to give you the basics needed to understand the economics of your business. Includes dozens of sample financial statements and rule-of-thumb formulas designed for non-accountants.

College Entrepreneur Handbook by Jonathan R. Aspatore
> A no-nonsense guide to planning, financing, and opening your own college-based business.

Develop & Market Your Creative Ideas by Dale A. Davis
> Details the many critical steps involved in transforming an idea into a successful business. Covers every facet from patents and trademarks, to test marketing, to financing and licensing.

Planning Your Business   (continued)

Location, Location, Location: How to Select the Best Site For Your Business
by Luigi Salvaneschi

Whether you are searching for a new business site or relocating an existing business, you have the power to dramatically increase or decrease your profits by choosing the right location. Discover how to discern a good location from a bad one, how to learn from your competition, and how understanding the retail trading zone can help you capture customers.

Retail in Detail by Ronald L. Bond

A hands-on guide written with warmth and humor, this book addresses such fundamentals as the best and worst aspects of retailing, site and name selection, store decor, bill paying, computerizing your accounting, managing your inventory, and more.

Selling Services by Paul O'Neil

If you are considering starting a consulting business, this practical handbook will help you to define and manage each stage of your business – from acquiring your first client to getting paid.

Start Your Business: A Beginner's Guide by PSI Research

An all-in-one resource for learning about general start-up requirements and preplanning activities. Features checklists, Plan of Action worksheets, a glossary of business terms and jargon, small business website index, and much more.

Business on the Internet

businessplan.com by L. Manning Ross

A leading-edge business tool that will help you produce a winning eCommerce business plan.

Connecting Online by Gregory R. Sherwin and Emily N. Avila

Teaches you how to promote your company, client, or not-for-profit organization through an Internet public relations strategy.

Web Wise by Sam Crowe

A simplified management guide for the development of a successful website. Learn how a novice Internet user can establish and maintain a presence on the web. An essential tool for anyone considering launching a business-related website.

Home-Based Business

Home Business Made Easy by David Hanania

This book is for anyone who wants to earn money working at home. Filled with fresh, new ideas for choosing and running a profitable and satisfying home business.

Moonlighting: Earn a Second Income at Home by Jo Frohbieter-Mueller

Learn how to determine which home-based business is best for you. Covers everything from assessing your interests and skills to how to pursue funding and maintain bookkeeping records.

Buying a Business

No Money Down Financing for Franchising by Roger C. Rule

Build a custom business plan that will get your franchise financed. Explore the financing resources available, many of which do not require any money down.

What's It Worth by Lloyd R. Manning

Discover the true value of a business before you buy or sell. Learn how real estate appraising works, why some appraisal methods should be preferred or avoided, and how to accurately measure sales, profit, and good will.

Preparing Your Business Plan

businessplan.com by L. Manning Ross

A leading-edge business tool that will help you produce a winning eCommerce business plan.

Location, Location, Location: How to Select the Best Site for Your Business by Luigi Salvaneschi

Whether you are searching for a new business site or relocating an existing business, you have the power to dramatically increase or decrease your profits by choosing the right location. Discover how to discern a good location from a bad one, how to learn from your competition, and how understanding the retail trading zone can help you capture customers.

The Rule Book of Business Plans for Startups by Roger Rule

Develop a customized business plan based on your industry type and eventual use. Whether you're starting a restaurant, retail or service business, home business or a non-profit, this book offers you the tools needed to start, expand, and raise capital.

Networking

Friendship Marketing by Gerald R. Baron

A practical guide to building your business by fostering better relationships. Learn from others who have successfully met the challenge of balancing a personal life with a professional one.

Successful Network Marketing for the 21st Century by Rod Nichold

An easy-to-follow guide for building a profitable network business from scratch. Includes information on how to choose the right company, prospecting, retailing, presentation, training and support, and more.

Financing Your Business

Financing Your Small Business by Art DeThomas

Learn how and where to successfully find additional money when your business needs it the most. Examines and explains financing fundamentals and alternatives in friendly, non-technical language.

Funding High-Tech Ventures by Richard L. Manweller

Show you how to obtain the funding needed to develop, produce, market, and sell high-tech products. Explains how to tailor your business plan strategy to attract potential investors.

No Money Down Financing for Franchising by Roger C. Rule

Build a custom business plan that will get your franchise financed. Explore the financing resources available, some not requiring any money down.

Small Business Insider's Guide to Bankers by Suzanne Caplan and Thomas M. Nunnally

Learn how to select the perfect bank and banker for your small business and maintain the relationship as your business evolves.

Bookkeeping and Financials

Business Owner's Guide to Accounting and Bookkeeping by José Placentia, Bruce Welge, and Don Oliver

Features clearly written, step-by-step instructions and practice situations to give you the basics needed to understand the economics of your business. Includes dozens of sample financial statements and rule-of-thumb formulas designed for non-accountants.

Financial Management Techniques for Small Business by Art DeThomas

Monitor and plan for your company's financial success. Shows you how to create and use income statements, balance sheets, cash flow statements, cash budgets, and much more.

Growing Your Business

Kick Ass Success: How to Achieve It by Joseph M. Sherlock

If you can't remember the last time you had fun at work, read this book! It's brimming with anecdotes and analogies to help you overcome the daily muck that keeps your company from succeeding.

Navigating the Marketplace: Growth Strategies for Your Business by Wayne Lovern and Anna Lovern

The practical guide to outsmarting the competition and increasing profits through the identification of a few critical marketing factors that affect sales and overhead. Learn five unique ways to target and satisfy five distinct types of customers. And much more.

Surviving Success: Managing the Challenges of Growth by Jeffrey A. Hansen

As a business grows, a company must learn to change and find different ways to maintain and expand the success. Learn how to take your business to the next level by adjusting priorities and establishing new organizational structures and cultures.

Advertising and Marketing

Advertising Without an Agency by Kathy J. Kobliski

A comprehensive guide to radio, television, print, direct mail, and outdoor advertising for small businesses.

Know Your Market: How to Do Low-Cost Market Research by David B. Frigstad

Implement a low-cost market research program and save time and money in the process. Provides worksheets, charts, tables and checklists designed with the small-business owner in mind.

Marketing for the New Millennium by Jay W. Tolman

Follow the example of successful brand-name companies and modernize your marketing efforts in the process. Covers Internet as well as more traditional forms such as direct mail, telemarketing, infomercials, and more.

Navigating the Marketplace: Growth Strategies for Your Business by Wayne and Anna Lovern

The practical guide to outsmarting the competition and increasing profits through the identification of a few critical marketing factors that affect sales and overhead. Learn five unique ways to target and satisfy five distinct types of customers. And much more.

Target $mart by Jay Newberg and Claudio Marcus

An action-oriented tool to increase customer purchases and attract new customers, while keeping your present customers coming back for more.

Sales and Customer Service

Delivering Legendary Customer Service by Richard S. Gallagher

> Learn how to get, keep, and grow customers for life by developing a full range of professional service skills. [a.k.a. *Smile Training Isn't Enough*]

Improving Staff Productivity by Ben Harrison Carter

> Learn how to identify and streamline your operations in order to increase your business' competitive edge and profits.

Keys to Leadership and Management Success

The Leader's Guide by Randall D. Ponder

> Learn the 15 essential skills every leader needs to master in order to lead a team to success. Helps you to understand what leadership is, how to develop a winning style, motivational techniques, and more.

Renaissance 2000: Liberal Arts Essential for Tomorrow's Leaders by Luigi Salvaneschi

> A revolutionary look at developing effective leadership skills through the pursuit of knowledge in the liberal arts. More than just theory, this groundbreaking book offers numerous techniques and exercises for improving one's ability to communicate with, and relate to, staff and peers alike. While most books will teach you practical means for honing professional, technical, and vocational skills, this one will show you why being a "whole" leader is the key to success.

More Tools for Success

Kick Ass Success: How to Achieve It by Joseph M. Sherlock

> If you can't remember the last time you had fun at work, read this book! It's brimming with anecdotes and analogies to help you overcome the daily muck that keeps your company from succeeding.

You Can't Go Wrong By Doing Right: 50 Principals for Running a Successful Business by Stephen L. Goldstein

> Learn how to be successful without resorting to today's slash-and-burn business practices. Explores fresh marketing and public relations strategies, classic customer service principles, and sure-fire management methods for creating a profitable and humane business.

Essential Corporation Handbook by Carl J. Sniffen

> Everything you want to know about operating your business as a corporation, but didn't know who to ask! This book takes the mystery out of corporate formalities, LLCs versus S-corporations, and more. Includes up-to-date information for all 50 states and the District of Columbia.

Acknowledgments

⏤

Never before have I experienced such an outpouring of support from complete strangers as I did for this book. Most of them had incredibly busy schedules, but they found the time to share the most intimate details of their business and personal lives. I am forever indebted to them for their candor and kindness. They are all wonderful, and some really stand out.

I want to thank Jenai Lane for her tireless encouragement. Each time we spoke, she suggested another name and offered more helpful tips. Even when she confided that she, too, is thinking about writing her own book on business, she continued to offer help for mine. In the world at large, it is all too common for people to hoard information, sharing with none but their confidants. But, these women believe in sharing the wealth. They take seriously their roles as mentors and role models.

Lynette Reed of Illume Candles, Inc. also made herself available at all costs, even sharing her most treasured picture of herself, pregnant with Isabelle, holding Harris in her candle factory. Lynette, like many of the women, spoke openly and honestly about her relationships, hopes, and fears. Often, I felt intrusive and a little embarrassed to be asking such personal questions, but they were all-giving. It is this spirit that makes the book so special. I want to thank Lynette's assistant, Diana, who never seemed to tire of playing phone tag, answering questions, and sending out information. Remarkably, she never seemed to have a bad day. Also, heartfelt thanks to Jennifer Maxwell and her assistant, Alyssa Berman, at PowerBar, Inc. for responding similarly to several requests. It is especially noteworthy that, while I was busily stalking Jennifer and Alyssa at PowerBar, Jennifer had her fifth baby.

Ed Moldt of the John PapaJohn Entrepreneurial Center at the University of Iowa deserves a huge thanks. In just one afternoon, while working on his own proposal, Ed Moldt talked with me for almost two hours about feasibility reports. His enthusiasm for entrepreneurialism and devotion to his students is boundless. He helped focus the book in a way I had not intended, and it is the better for it.

Additional thanks must be given to his student entrepreneur, Tara Cronbaugh of the Iowa City Coffee House. She not only gave generously of her time, she allowed a good look at her behind-the-scene progress and mistakes.

Admittedly, I was a little star-struck when I spoke with J'Amy Owens. She exudes such confidence and poise, I found myself both befuddled and honored by her patience and generosity. When I found the budding business of Stacey Center, Owens agreed — for free — to analyze the business. Center was stunned by Owens' gracious gift.

A great deal of love and care have been devoted to this book by the folks at The Oasis Press. Everyone worked so hard to make this a reality, but a special thanks must go to the publishers Emmett and Ardella Ramey and to my editor, designer, and personal connection C.C. Dickinson, whose voice over the phone became as familiar and welcomed as any family member's.

Of my family, each and every one played an important role. Most of this book was written with our family guinea pig, Penny, sitting on my shoulder. As long as Penny sat on my shoulder, nibbling on my collar, my eldest daughter was content that I was part of the game and left me to my work. (I suppose I should also thank Penny for doing nothing more than nibbling my collar while sitting on my shoulder.) And, thanks to my children, I learned to budget time and become more focused. And, because of my children, I learned to value things in a different, better way: time, friendships, what's really important in life.

My parents have been and continue to be instrumental in my writing career. Simply put, without them, there would be no books. They taught me to believe in myself, to love myself, and aim high. As always, my sister, Michelle, acted as friend, editor, and sounding board. Even when she was going through some particularly hard times of her own, she never stopped being a supportive, grounding force in my always hectic life. And to my dear husband, Robb, who listened to me rant and rave as I experienced computer difficulties, thanks honey; your patience was worth more than gold.

In the seventh month of my third pregnancy, as I was closing in on the end of this book, the manuscript was entirely lost. It was a horrible, devastating experience, and since I was hormonally on the edge as it was, I was not someone to be around. Yet my friends and family rallied around me. While Robb and lifelong-friend Mark Larkin spent hours working on the computer in hopes of salvaging the damage (ultimately the computer was replaced with a new one), it was my mother who came to the rescue.

Acting as editor, she'd saved an old hardcopy from which I could begin the rebuilding process. And when entrepreneur and dear friend Tess Rano learned what had happened, she cried with me. Admittedly, she had never written more than five pages of anything and had no idea how much time and effort was put into 250-plus pages of research and interviews, but she knew it was something important to me. Above all, I want to thank my mother. As is discussed in the book, she instilled in me the importance of mentoring, friendship, and dreaming.

It is because of these people: family, friends, and newly acquired business relationships that this book was born, developed, reborn again, and completed. Words cannot say enough thanks.

One day, my editor C.C. and I were talking about the women in the book when she told me she sensed, while reading, that I genuinely liked the women I interviewed. I do, each and every one. How lucky I am to have worked, however briefly, with such a diverse group of thoroughly delightful and generous women.

Lastly, thank you, dear reader, for picking up this book and delving into the magical world of hopes and dreams. Let's hope you can make more of it than just hopes and dreams.

Good luck in your ventures.

Index